THE ASSAULT ON FORT BLAKELEY

The Thunder and Lightning of Battle

MIKE BUNN

THE History PRESS

Published by The History Press
Charleston, SC
www.historypress.com

Front cover: *The Battle of Fort Blakeley*, by Rick Reeves.

First published 2021

Manufactured in the United States

ISBN 9781467148634

Library of Congress Control Number: 2020948446

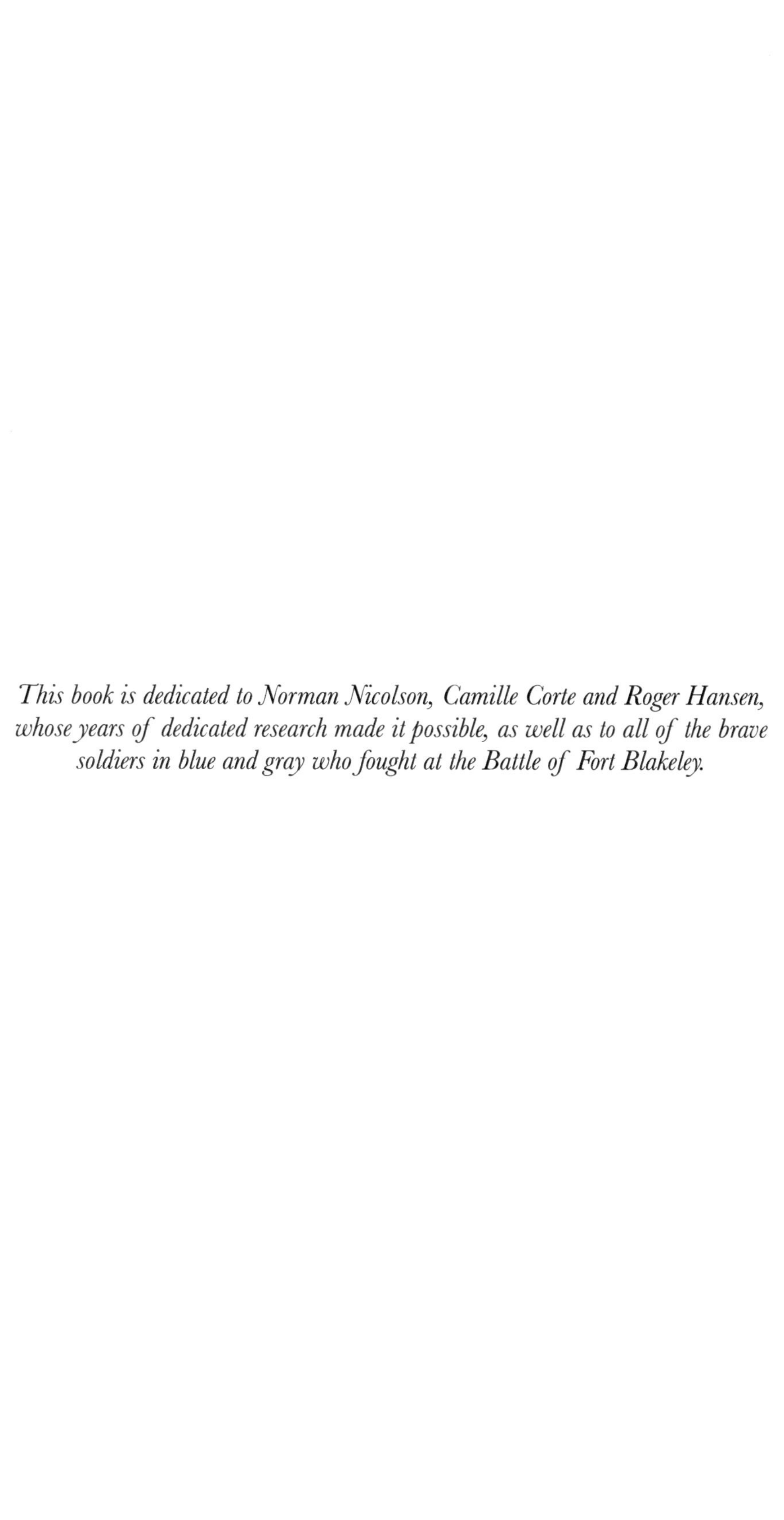

This book is dedicated to Norman Nicolson, Camille Corte and Roger Hansen, whose years of dedicated research made it possible, as well as to all of the brave soldiers in blue and gray who fought at the Battle of Fort Blakeley.

Contents

Preface

The Battle of Fort Blakeley was the largest open-field Civil War battle fought in the state of Alabama and one of the last of the entire war. On the afternoon of Sunday, April 9, 1865, some 16,000 Union troops stepped out of their trenches after a weeklong siege featuring constant skirmishing to launch a coordinated assault on a three-mile-wide Confederate line defended by about 3,500 troops. It was one of the grand spectacles of the war and the climax of the combined-forces campaign aimed at the capture of the city of Mobile. The fall of Blakeley led directly to the surrender of the last major Southern city to remain Confederate hands.

Today, Historic Blakeley State Park preserves and interprets the story of that battle. The park contains the great majority of the remarkably intact Confederate and Union earthen lines that figured in the siege and battle, making it one of the best-preserved Civil War battlefields in the nation. Interpretive signage along with printed and audio guides help visitors discover the battlefield, and the park's regular living history programming, tours, lectures and boat cruises assist in communicating to the public what happened on its grounds and its significance in the war's last major campaign.

I have been privileged to serve as the director of Historic Blakeley State Park for the past several years, and it has been my honor to help develop interpretation of the battle for a variety of self-guided touring options, as well to guide thousands of visitors on explorations of the park's many points of historical interest. By boat, in walking and riding tours, as well as in countless presentations to civic groups, students and the general public,

I have shared Blakeley's story. The more I became involved in telling about the battle, though, the more I became acutely aware that nothing communicated the essence of the fight better than the words of those who actually fought in the contest. The raw emotion of the experience of combat, the natural fear and unexpected heroism of the soldiers in blue and gray, the pride in duty fulfilled and faithful service rendered for cause and comrades and the maelstrom of the earth-pounding sound and thick, swirling smoke of battle I can scarcely convey as well as the reports, diaries, letters and memoirs of the Battle of Fort Blakeley's participants that I have relied on in my interpretive efforts.

That knowledge and my desire to create a more comprehensive understanding of the battle for visitors and help them form an emotional connection with the soldiers who took part in the grand drama we interpret at the park led to the genesis of this book. It is not a traditional narrative history—for that, I recommend readers consult the good works of park friend Paul Brueske (*The Last Siege*), Sean Michael O'Brien (*Mobile, 1865*), Chester Hearn (*Mobile Bay and the Mobile Campaign*), Russell Blount Jr. (*Besieged: Mobile 1865*) or the first work on the campaign to appear in print just a year after its conclusion, Christopher C. Andrews's *History of the Campaign of Mobile*, among others. Rather, I have arranged this work like an extended guided tour, briefly providing the contextual information on the circumstances of the battle's occurrence. Then, in a series of quick-moving chapters, I provide an overview of the fight sector by sector. I approach interpretation of the battle much as a visitor would approach touring the land where it happened, going zone by zone to understand what occurred in each area. The focus is on the drama-filled twenty to thirty minutes of the charge on Fort Blakeley on the evening of Sunday, April 9, 1865, moments where the lives of many were lost and that others would remember for the rest of theirs. I provide a brief bit of background on various units of participants who left compelling written accounts of the battle and then feature quotes from the men who later wrote or were interviewed about their experience. I have purposefully chosen to let veterans of the Battle of Fort Blakeley speak for themselves in this way instead of attempting to fit portions of their words into quotes buried in a narrative of my own creation about those chaotic events. I hope this allows their voices to be more clearly heard. It is my goal that this strategy will facilitate the reader's connection to the amazing historic site that is the battlefield at Historic Blakeley State Park in a unique way, whether they enjoy it in the comfort of their living room or use it as a guide in touring the park on their own.

Readers will note there are considerably more accounts from the Union soldiers who fought at Blakeley than Confederate. This is for good reason. There were nearly five times as many Federal troops on the battlefield as Rebels. Also, because virtually the entire garrison of the fort was either killed in action or captured and sent to prisons to wait out the end of the war, the Southerners issued no official after-action reports. Precious few contemporary letters home describing the affair from their viewpoint were written or survive. This book also does not include every account of the battle to be found. The edited accounts showcased here are among the most evocative I have found and were selected for their vivid descriptions of combat, their representativeness as a sample of the experience of soldiers in the fight at Blakeley, or both.

In compiling them, I drew extensively on the good work of Norman Nicolson, who over a period of decades as a labor of love gathered what is probably the most comprehensive collection of information on the Battle of Fort Blakeley ever assembled. A Mobile native and lifelong student of history, Nicolson was educated as an engineer and spent more than three decades working in the shipping industry. His work investigating the battle at Blakeley consumed an enormous amount of his free time. He was assisted at various points in the latter stages of his research by park employee Camille Corte and fellow researcher, reenactor and park friend Roger Hansen. Nicolson's collection is today housed at the Historic Mobile Preservation Society's Minnie Mitchell Archives on the Oakleigh campus in midtown Mobile. It contains copies of dozens of accounts of the battle in the form of copies Nicolson obtained from archives elsewhere, published accounts and a few copies of letters that he obtained from descendants of veterans directly. Wherever possible, I have cited the repository in which the original documents are held or the publication in which they first appeared in this book. To this veritable treasure chest of information I added some findings of my own from a variety of other sources: regional archives, official records, unpublished maps, rare images and, of course, walking and discovering the land itself. I want to extend a special thanks to Bob Peck, longtime volunteer at the Mitchell Archives and an incredible resource on local history, for helping arrange access to the Nicolson Collection over the course of two years of intensive research.

Admittedly, Fort Blakeley in no way figured as prominently in Confederate defeat as, say, the Battle of Gettysburg or the capture of Vicksburg. Still, the story of the fight at Blakeley is nonetheless significant and compelling in its own right. It is one of only two "Class A" battlefields in Alabama as designated by the Civil War Sites Advisory Commission, meaning the fighting that took place there played a decisive role in determining the outcome of a major strategic objective of the war. But further than that, the Battle of Fort Blakeley is the Gulf Coast's centerpiece connection to the type of large-scale combat that decided the course of events in the cataclysmic turning point in American history of which it was a part. Its story is filled with examples of the types of bravery and action that accompany every noteworthy clash of the war. It involved real people laying their lives on the line in pitched battle, hundreds of whom perished in the undertaking. The fight is relatively little known today and frequently dismissed as an inconsequential mopping-up operation owing to the fact that it occurred on the very day General Robert E. Lee surrendered his Army of Northern Virginia at Appomattox. I believe it to be a disservice to those who fought here to treat it as a sideshow—what the men who fought in the battle endured was anything but irrelevant in their lives or to the region they grappled for control of. This characterization contributes to an oversimplified understanding of the war. The Civil War, after all, was a shared national saga, but one that played out in hundreds of local events guided by the decisions and actions of hundreds of thousands of individuals. By reading the words of those who fought at Blakeley, one gains an appreciation for the fact that, regardless of what might be happening elsewhere, their focus and commitment was on the job at hand, and they went to it with abandon.

I believe there is a certain unmistakable but ephemeral power evoked by the experience of visiting the sites where human drama unfolded. I am not referring to any supernatural phenomena—although if spirits do haunt the places where lives were changed or lost in large numbers, Blakeley would surely have its share—but rather to a compelling and visceral connection with visitors once they know a little of what people endured at a given location, of what they saw and heard, of what they took away from an event and, ultimately, if they lived through it or not. I invite you to use the pages of narrative that follow, then, to come along with Blakeley's veterans into the camps and trenches of the battlefield and across its hallowed grounds on the last grand charge of the Civil War. I hope this publication helps you understand what took place along the banks of the Tensaw on April 9, 1865, and awakens you to the import of the incredible story Historic Blakeley State Park preserves.

Chapter 1

The Siege of Fort Blakeley

In the spring of 1865, Mobile stood as the largest Southern city outside of Richmond still in Confederate hands. Although it had been shut off from international commercial ports and its period of significance as a blockade-running haven had come to an end with the Confederate defeat at the Battle of Mobile Bay in August 1864, Mobile still held strategic importance as a vital transportation and supply hub to what remained of the Confederacy. Union military authorities determined its capture to be one of the major goals of the fifth spring of campaigning in a war that they appeared to be winning but was far from over. The Battle of Fort Blakeley would ultimately become the key contest in the war's last major campaign.[1]

Federal authorities had Mobile in their sights long before the spring of 1865, but other objectives prevented the concentration of men and material necessary for the mission. As early as 1862, immediately after the fall of New Orleans, Admiral David G. Farragut had wanted to move on the port city. Pressing needs for naval duty along the Mississippi forced the delay of the effort. General Ulysses S. Grant had considered some sort of movement into the interior of Alabama, where several iron production facilities and the sprawling ordnance production center at Selma were located, in the fall of 1863. Other operations, though, once again put those plans on hold before they got started.

After Grant's elevation to command of all Union armies in 1864, Mobile again came into his crosshairs. The logistical needs of the Red River campaign—a combined-forces operation into central Louisiana in the

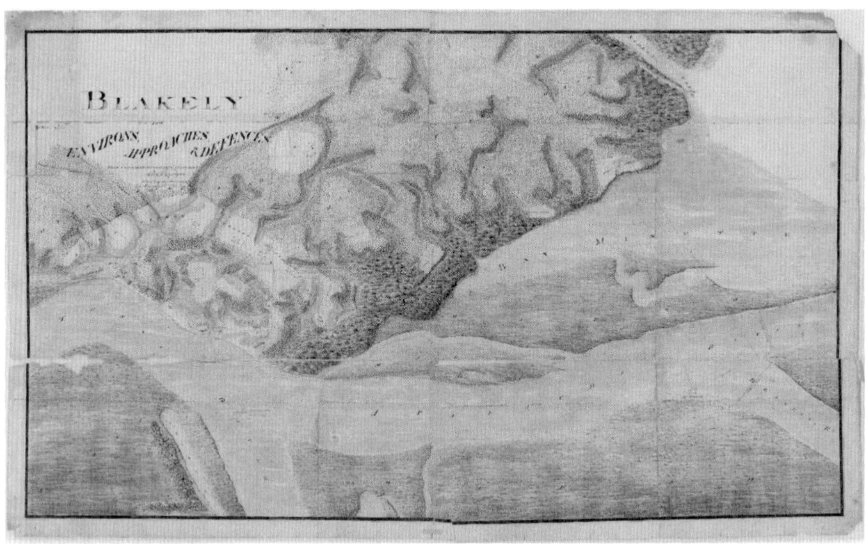

This section of a map of Blakeley's defenses was produced a short time prior to the siege by artist and engineer Nicola Marschall, the man generally credited with having created the design for the first Confederate national flag. Marschall executed the plan at the order of Colonel Samuel Lockett, chief engineer for the Department of Alabama, Mississippi and East Louisiana. *National Archives.*

spring of 1864 advocated by Union general in chief Henry W. Halleck and featuring more than thirty thousand troops and a squadron of gunboats—forced yet another postponement of plans for taking Mobile, however. The Red River expedition was an abject failure from the Union perspective, accomplishing none of its objectives and, in the mind of Grant, causing a maddening delay in his plans for capturing Mobile, Selma and the politically significant city of Montgomery, the first capital of the Confederacy. Shortly after winning the Battle of Mobile Bay in August 1864, Admiral Farragut had conducted a reconnaissance of the city's waterside defenses by sailing up to within about three miles of the city with a squadron of gunboats. He took careful notes on all the engineering the Confederates had performed and lobbed a few shells at the outer batteries protecting it and a Confederate ship anchored behind them to precious little effect. He promptly withdrew, convinced that only a substantial combined force and a protracted siege could bring about the capture of Mobile, remarking that it would be "an elephant and take a large army to hold it."[2]

By the fall of 1864, Grant had determined to finally move ahead with planning for assembling the resources necessary for a campaign against Mobile. Not only would its primary objective serve the goals of the Union

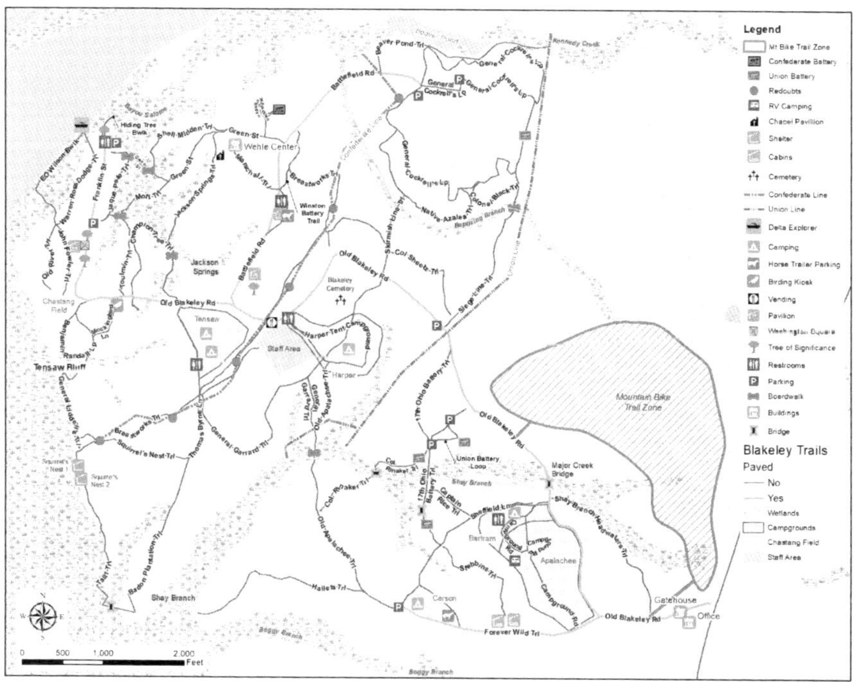

Map of Historic Blakeley State Park today. *Historic Blakeley State Park.*

war effort directly, but opening up action in the Gulf Coast theater would also potentially divert Confederate resources from other efforts in the lower South, such as the operations of General William T. Sherman, not to mention prevent General Robert E. Lee from receiving any resources from the region while Grant faced him in Virginia. To help ensure its success, a major cavalry raid into central Alabama, led by Brigadier General James H. Wilson, was to take place simultaneously with the advance of a combined force of navy and infantry along the Gulf Coast. Grant tapped Major General Edward S. Canby for the mission.

A forty-seven-year-old Kentucky native, Canby was a veteran with a long record of solid service. He had seen action in the Second Seminole War, the Mexican-American War and in numerous posts in the Civil War from New Mexico and New York to the Gulf South by the time of this assignment. Owing to an abundance of caution, and perhaps a touch of slowness due to a prolonged recovery from a painful and slightly embarrassing wound received in the Red River expedition (he had taken in bullet squarely in the rear end that tore through his thigh before exiting but somehow missing major blood vessels), Canby took what seemed to Grant an inordinate amount of time to initiate his campaign. Grant, ready to replace him if he did not act, sternly commanded him in early March to cease with preparation and to "take Mobile and hold it, and push our forces to the interior to Montgomery and Selma." Canby was making final arrangements for the expedition when the note arrived. Only a week later, he had his men in motion.[3]

Mobile ranked as one of the most heavily fortified cities in North America by the spring of 1865. Four years of preparation for any potential attack had yielded multiple lines of defense. A series of several miles of earthworks ringed the city and protected its landward approaches. Along the waterways where the rivers of the Mobile-Tensaw Delta emptied into Mobile Bay were several batteries where large-caliber cannons could be brought to bear on any approaching enemy ships. Pilings had been placed within river channels so as to force boats attempting to ply their waters into narrow, navigable passages directly within range of these guns. Confederates had also laced some of these waterways with floating mines, called torpedoes at the time. A small but substantial flotilla of gunboats, including three well-armed ironclads, in theory stood at the ready to move to any spot where they were needed. Even though not all of them had engines strong enough to reliably stem the currents of the rivers they were to protect, they promised to be a formidable obstacle for any approaching enemy force on land or water.[4]

Opposite Mobile, along the eastern shores of the delta guarding access to the deep and wide Tensaw River and its distributaries, stood two massive artillery-studded earthen fortifications known as Spanish Fort and Fort Blakeley, where more than half of the nearly nine thousand troops at the disposal of department commander Major General Dabney H. Maury were stationed. Yale-educated lawyer and Louisiana planter Brigadier General Randall L. Gibson commanded at Spanish Fort. A veteran of the campaigns of the Western Theater, he had seen hard fighting at Shiloh, Chickamauga and Atlanta prior to arriving on the banks of Mobile Bay. Another Louisiana planter, St. John Richardson Lidell, held overall command at Blakeley. He had attended but not graduated from West Point, but he distinguished himself as a competent and bold leader in actions throughout the Western Theater prior to his posting in defense of Mobile. Between their posts and Mobile, guarding approach to the city via the tangle of waterways where the delta met the bay, stood two stout artillery positions known as Battery Huger and Battery Tracy. Any operation planned against Mobile clearly needed to be large and draw on the resources of both the army and the navy to have any chance of success, and it would likely suffer considerable casualties in the undertaking regardless.[5]

Combining forces already in place at Fort Gaines and Fort Morgan with elements of the XVI Corps and troops stationed at Pensacola, Canby would have nearly forty-five thousand men with which to conduct the campaign. Those troops included: the XIII Corps, under overall command of General Gordon Granger, thirteen thousand men in three divisions; the XVI Corps, under overall command of Major General A.J. Smith, sixteen thousand men in three divisions; a column at Pensacola under the command of Major General Frederick Steele, thirteen thousand men; Brigadier General Thomas J. Lucas's cavalry; several units of artillery; and a few companies of engineers. Of these forces, Canby would eventually send some sixteen thousand men to reduce Blakeley: the 1st Division of the United States Colored Troops (USCT) under Brigadier General John P. Hawkins, the 1st Division of the XIII Corps under Brigadier General James C. Veatch, the 2nd Division of the XIII Corps under Brigadier General Christopher C. Andrews and the 2nd Division of the XVI Corps under Brigadier General Kenner Garrard. Many of the troops in these ranks comprised rugged midwestern units with significant combat experience, including early war actions in the mountains of Arkansas, service in the pitched battles and long siege of the Vicksburg campaign, the smaller fights and ignominious setbacks in the swamps of the Red River in Louisiana and the devastating assault on the Confederate line on wintry December days in front of Nashville.[6]

While Grant had entrusted Canby with rather wide latitude in devising strategies to accomplish the mission laid out for him, he had made a few priorities clear. Mobile was to be the first major target of the campaign, and its capture was, of course, highly desired. But if it could not be affected without an extended siege, Canby was to bypass the city and move on toward Selma and Montgomery, as he considered them the more strategically important objectives. The cautious Canby could not countenance leaving even a small Rebel army with potential to control access to the rivers into the interior in his rear and determined to clear Confederate forces from the Mobile Bay area and capture the city of Mobile before moving on. The result was that he ended up fighting perhaps a more extended siege than Grant would have liked to accomplish this first goal in not one but two locations, and Wilson's cavalry ended up taking Selma and Montgomery by itself. Canby determined to reduce the fortifications on the Eastern Shore and then, having gained control of the waterways they protected, launch an amphibious attack on the relatively unprotected eastern flank of Mobile.[7]

Canby could not execute his plans without significant naval support, and the campaign for Mobile was a true combined-forces operation. In February 1865, Admiral Henry Knox Thatcher, who had taken command of the West Gulf Blockading Squadron in January 1865, arrived in Mobile Bay to assume command of Union naval forces to coordinate with Canby. His fleet numbered over thirty warships, including gunboats and ironclad monitors that had taken part in Battle of Mobile Bay, as well as a number of other smaller transport boats. By the end of the campaign, nine Federal vessels would be lost, most due to the floating mines or "torpedoes" Confederate engineers had laced throughout the watery approaches to Spanish Fort and Blakeley. More than two hundred sailors would be wounded or killed in the waters of the lower Mobile-Tensaw Delta during March and April 1865. While Thatcher's tars suffered a disproportionate share of casualties in the operation, they rendered invaluable service transporting troops, ferrying supplies and conducting reconnaissance operations in addition to shelling Confederate positions along the Eastern Shore.[8]

The army, meanwhile, moved on the Eastern Shore defenses at Spanish Fort and Fort Blakeley in two large columns. Some thirty-two thousand men under Canby's direct command moved through western and central Baldwin County toward their objective. Breaking camp on the morning of March 17, the XIII Corps marched east, over the Fort Morgan peninsula, before turning north at what is now the Gulf Shores, Alabama. In the meantime, the XVI Corps began a crossing of Mobile Bay from Fort Gaines by boats on March 19. A brigade of the XVI Corps was sent on a feint toward Mobile before rejoining the main column. The two corps met at the mouth of Fish River on Weeks Bay to continue their advance together. General Steele's column began its movement from Pensacola simultaneously, heading north out of town with nearly thirteen thousand men and some 250 wagons creaking toward the Alabama state line.[9]

Although the terrain over which the armies traveled was relatively level over much of the route, long sections proved to be a difficult, muddy slog for both columns as they advanced through fields and forests saturated by recent rains. "The march was a severe one on the men," remembered Brigadier General John P. Hawkins, "being attended with constant labor, making corduroy roads to get the wagons through the almost impassable swamps." "Wagons sank in the sand to the hub, after rain," observed one Illinois soldier, causing the men to occasionally halt to push, pull and drag their heavy equipment through the muck. Draft animals were used to help keep the

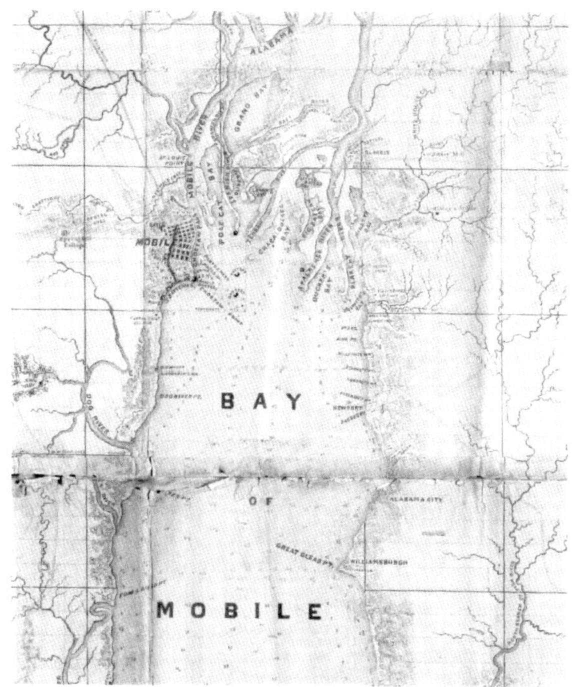

Left: Map of the Defenses of Mobile and Vicinity in 1863, prepared by order of Major General Nathaniel P. Banks prior to the construction of Fort Blakeley. *Library of Congress.*

Below: Defenses of Mobile in 1865. *Library of Congress.*

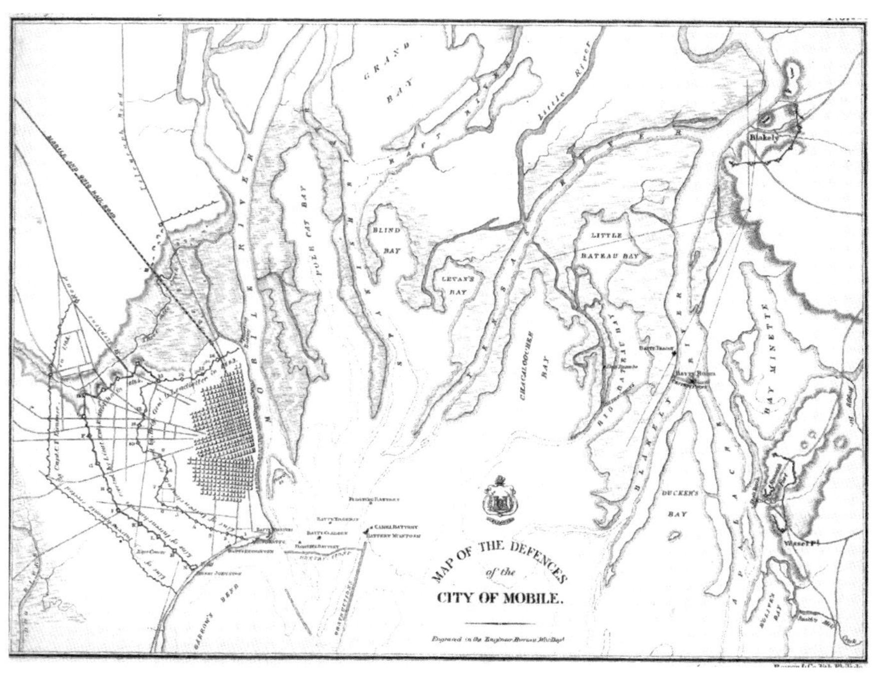

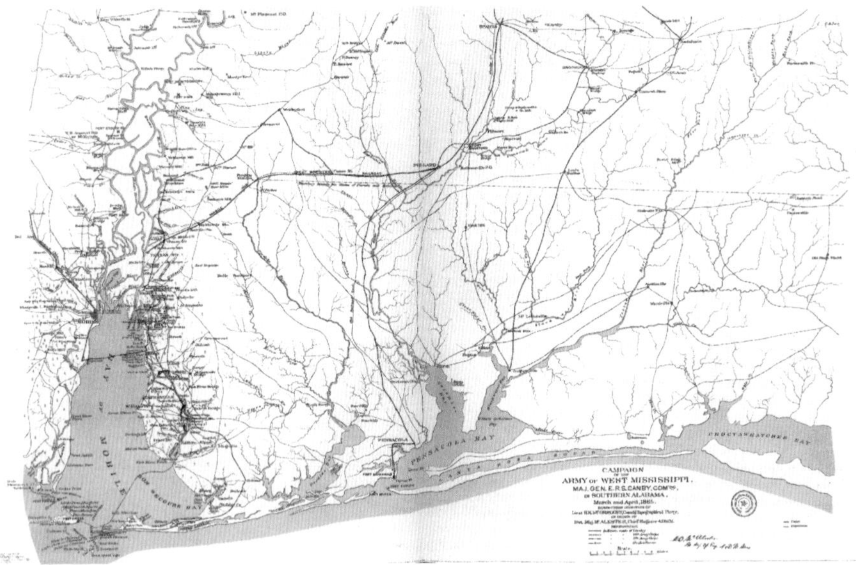

Map of troop movements in the campaign for Mobile that appeared in the *Atlas to Accompany the Official Records of the Union and Confederate Armies*. *Library of Congress.*

trains moving, but even they became mired at times. When the quadrupeds got stuck, according to one sarcastic soldier of the 35th Wisconsin, "then we pull the donkeys, mud up to our knees, but those longears weren't dumb. When things didn't move, they layed down....We two-legged ones with the back pack and three-day ration on our backs had to pull the carts out of the mud." It was, in the estimation of one trooper, simply "the worst country I ever saw for an Army to march through." Making their situation all the more melancholy, many regiments began to run low on rations during the extended journey. Some reported going at least thirty-six hours with no food, the march taking longer than had been planned and logistical difficulties of the situation making resupply a herculean task. On the whole, the march to Blakeley proved to be a miserable, slow trek.[10]

The advance was not without incidents of peril either. Small-scale skirmishing became nearly constant in Canby's front from Fish River onward. The cavalry in the van of Steele's column, which feinted a thrust northward into central Alabama before turning southward and plunging down on the position at Blakeley, fought several small skirmishes with Confederate forces contesting stream crossings as it moved. In short, spirited fights at sluggish streams known as Cotton Creek, Mitchell Creek, Canoe Creek and Pritchett Mill Branch, stubborn Rebel cavalry did their best to slow the Federal forces

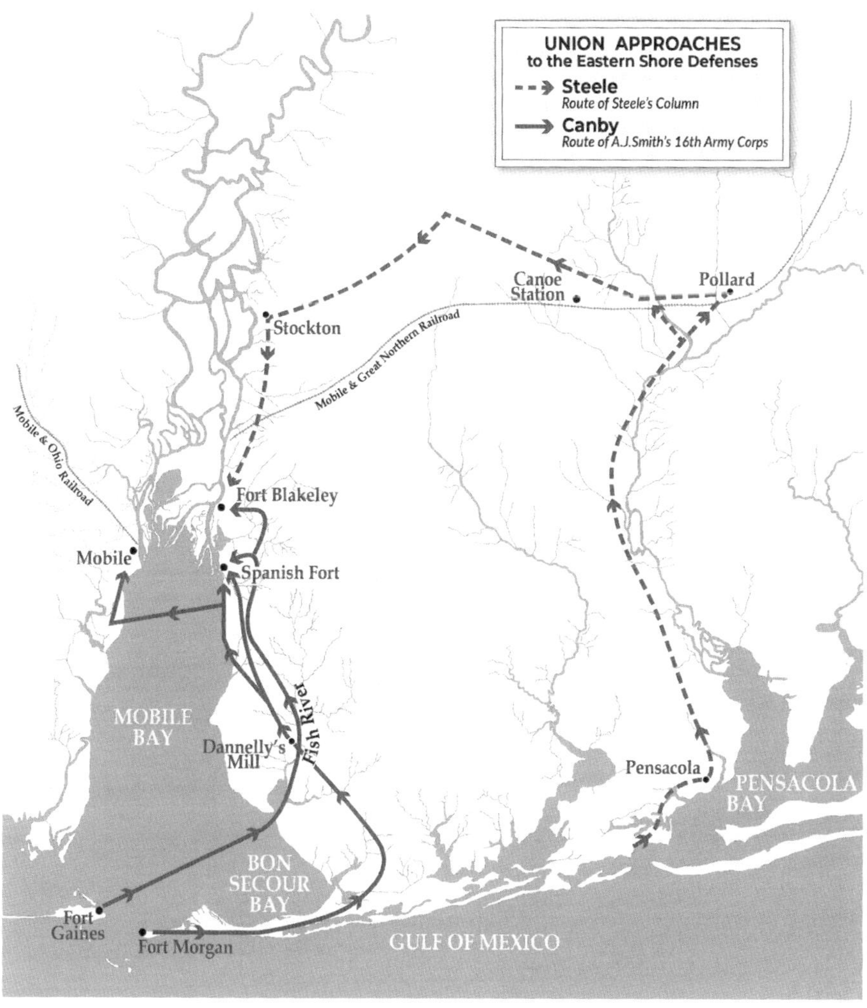

Map showing the route of Canby and Steele's men. *Historic Blakeley State Park.*

in a running firefight. Steele's command, vastly outnumbering its foes, inexorably pushed onward despite the resistance.

Horsemen in both columns discovered the true measure of the lengths the Rebels were willing to go to defend their position on the roads just outside Blakeley. They buried landmines, called torpedoes or sub-terra shells at the time, in the road itself. When unsuspecting horses stepped on these devices, the results could be catastrophic. A few horses were killed, along with at least one rider, on the Stockton Road in this manner. Jonathan Merriam of the 117th Illinois narrowly escaped an untimely demise when he encountered a mine in the road just south of Blakeley on his way up from around Spanish Fort on April 2, 1865. "I was riding by the side of Gen. Gilbert on his left and his Adjutant General on his right and three other officers were riding in the same way right behind us," he remembered in his after-action report. "One of the horses trod upon a torpedo exploding it with a frightful concussion. Blinded by the smoke and sand and stunned by the terrific explosion we staggered like drunken men. I realized in a moment that I was not killed but for some moments could not comprehend what had happened." Two of the horses the men were riding were instantly slain. "That we were not all killed is certainly a wonder and that none were seriously hurt is more than strange....I regard it as the narrowest escape of my life....I have not got all the sand out of my ears yet."[11]

Baldwin County at the time was a relatively sparsely populated region of small farms and modest communities, far from the primary areas of cotton production in the central areas of Alabama. It had a total population of only about 7,500 people, roughly half of them enslaved. At least in part owing to this, the Yankee army's track across the county was not marked with a wide swath of destruction similar to some others engrained in Civil War lore. But plunder and destruction of private property did occur as the blue columns moved toward Blakeley. "Burned Hall's house. Tore up the railroad and the telegraph wire and poles," recorded one soldier in the 76th Illinois of a day's work on the march through Baldwin County. As Steele's men advanced, they confiscated whatever stashes of corn they ran across and conducted a virtual raid on the community of Stockton. Local legend in Montrose and Daphne, Eastern Shore communities just a few miles south of Blakeley, recounts how the Federals helped themselves to valuables when the opportunity presented itself. At the home of Sarah Louisa Graham, for example, soldiers took food, the family's lone horse, furniture and silver. Acting on a tip from a slave, they even dug up jewelry that had been buried in hopes of escaping detection. While a few scattered accounts of slaves emancipating themselves to offer their services to the invading army have been found in accounts of the campaign for Mobile, it is unclear how many attempted to flee at the sight of the Federal army or to what degree, if any, their services were officially utilized. How much property was similarly destroyed or repurposed by the invading armies marching through Baldwin County may never be known, but the amount appears relatively small. As they swept through the village of Daphne, in fact, a band of Federals took the time to request permission to sleep in the still extant Methodist church from the widow of its builder. Despite her proud declaration to them that she was a Rebel "from the top of my head to the bottom of my feet!" the men did no harm to the structure.[12]

Leading elements of Canby's column began arriving at a sluggish stream known as D'Olive Creek, which empties into Mobile Bay about a mile south of the earthworks at Spanish Fort, on March 26, 1865. The Confederates stationed there had destroyed the bridge over the stream, planted torpedoes along its approaches and came out to threaten attack. They deployed along the hillside opposite the waterway, under the assumption that they faced only a portion of the Federal army and might halt their advance near the stream crossing. Quickly realizing that they faced a much larger force that would soon outnumber them many times over, they decided to make an orderly withdrawal into their fortifications rather than make a stand in the open field. In the process, Rebel forces destroyed the bridge over Minette Bay, on the road to Blakeley, just as elements of the Union army attempted to flank their position by approaching it from the east. Heavy skirmishing rang out in the woods near Sibley's Mill just three miles south of Blakeley in the last days of March, a prelude to what would become the systematic investment of Spanish Fort and a harbinger of what lay in store for Fort Blakeley.[13]

The Confederate line at Spanish Fort stretched for more than two miles along the Blakeley River. Manned by about 2,500 troops and dozens of pieces of artillery, it was a formidable position guarding against approach to Mobile via the east or the gaining of entry into the Mobile-Tensaw Delta river system via its eastern waterways. It was no match for the combined-forces efforts of the Union army and navy, however, which could bring to bear more than 30,000 troops, some ninety pieces of artillery and more than a dozen gunboats in the environs. Its siege stretched out nearly two weeks, as the Federal forces gathered so close to the Rebel fort and kept up such a continual barrage of shot and shell that its defenders could scarcely return fire themselves. When, on the evening of April 8, Federals severed a portion of the left flank of the Confederate line, Brigadier General Gibson ordered a stealthy evacuation of the post under cover of dark lest his entire force be surrounded and captured the next morning. Thus Canby's men gained what they felt was a hollow victory when on the morning of April 9, 1865, they awoke to find Spanish Fort in their possession but its army vanished. They would take pains to avoid a similar result at Fort Blakeley, about four miles to the north, whose siege had gotten underway just a few days after the investment of Spanish Fort had begun.[14]

Blakeley had at one point been one of the largest towns in the state of Alabama, and its founders worked hard to make it a commercial rival to Mobile in the early years of its existence. Its heyday had come and gone some four decades prior to the siege and battle to which it lent its name, however; by the time Confederate and Union troops squared off in the fields surrounding its site, Blakeley was little more than a sleepy village with only a handful of permanent residents. It therefore stood as a virtual ghost town in 1865. "Blakeley is a small town…better located as regards health (than Mobile), and the eastern channel can float larger craft than the western. But really, Blakeley is just no place at all," observed a reporter for the *New York Times* sent to cover the campaign for Mobile. True enough, the community, or what remained of it, had little to do with the selection of the site as a point of defense for the city of Mobile by Confederate authorities. Rather, the stretch of high ground along the Tensaw in its environs and its deepwater port at the intersection of the Stockton and Pensacola Roads made the place strategically important as a point of concentration for men and materials.[15]

The first Federal units had arrived in the vicinity of the defenses at Blakeley on April 1. Rebel cavalry posted on the outskirts of the fortification scouting for enemy approach had engaged the leading elements of the Federal army along the roads leading to the town, opening the contest that would become the weeklong siege of Fort Blakeley. Major Ephraim Brown of the 114th Ohio recorded that his regiment encountered one such band of Rebels as they neared the fort: "Our cavalry made a dash on them and gobbled them in, almost every man, numbering about 250. This opened the ball." In one of these skirmishes, perhaps the same, Captain R.N. Rea was out on patrol with the body servant of a fellow officer when they spotted Yankee cavalry and made a narrow escape representative of several close calls on the outer reaches of the Confederate lines. "I could hear the little negro boy say: 'Go it, massa! They are about to get us.'…I thought so too," he remembered. "On we went like a prairie fire and finally came to Cockrell's brigade." The bluecoats brushed aside the thin skirmish lines like Rea's in short order and began concentrating about a mile away from the Confederate fortifications in the first days of April 1865. Their proximity forced the fort's defenders behind their lines; General Lidell up until that point had maintained his headquarters at a house perched atop a bluff on the road just north of Blakeley, and some of his men had been camping on the open ground in front of their works.[16]

As Federal units took position in front of Fort Blakeley, they got their first look at the menacing earthen fortification. Stretching three miles in

The New-York Times.

NEW-YORK, MONDAY, APRIL 24, 1865.

VOL. XIV......NO. 4237.

THE CAMPAIGN IN ALABAMA.

The Capture of Mobile and All Its Defences.

Immense Captures of Artillery and Stores.

Details of the Assault on Spanish Fort.

THE BATTLE OF BLAKELY.

The Rebel General Clanton Killed, and Gens. Lyddell, Thomas, and Cockerell Captured.

Fifteen Hundred Rebels Killed and Wounded and Six Thousand Prisoners.

Federal Loss Eighteen Hundred Killed and Wounded.

Full Particulars of the Whole Campaign.

The campaign for Mobile made front-page news as far away as New York. *From the* New York Times, *April 24, 1865. Library of Congress.*

a broad arc connecting on the north and south with the Tensaw River, the interconnected line was studded with nearly forty pieces of frowning artillery and some 3,500 troops. Almost the entirety of its length could clearly be seen by the Yankee troopers, as the Rebels, using hundreds of impressed slaves, had caused virtually all the timber in front of the fort to be cleared for several hundred yards. This open ground Fort Blakeley's defenders meant to serve as a killing field. Not only would anyone daring approach come within range of Rebel guns, but all manner of obstructions defied easy approach as well. The timber felled to create these fields of fire lay strewn across the expansive void between the wood line and the Confederate parapet. Closer in were rows of abatis formed from the tops of the trees that had been felled; negotiating this tangle of debris on foot while under fire promised to be a hazardous duty indeed. Rows of substantial rifle pits, where squads of skirmishers could be placed as an around-the-clock alarm system and first line of defense, guarded against any surprise attack and added another layer of danger to any planned assault. Unbeknownst to the Federals upon arrival, the Rebels had also stealthily strung telegraph wire between some of the stumps of the trees that had been cut down—a trip hazard that might bring an entire column of unsuspecting attackers to a disorderly halt while under the guns of the fort. Beyond all this, just a few dozen yards from the

Above and opposite: These images of abatis, tangled felled trees and cheveaux de frise in front of Atlanta help us understand how the battlefield at Blakeley would have appeared at the time of the siege. *Library of Congress.*

main line in front of the redoubts, or mini-forts where artillery and troops were concentrated, was a row of sharpened stakes with ominous points bristling defiance to the intruders. Each was joined by a substantial line of entrenchments that made Fort Blakeley one sprawling, interconnected line of earthworks. On the sides of selected redoubts stood *cheveaux de frise*, a medieval-looking piece of maneuverable defensive engineering made from sharpened poles arranged around a center beam that could bring to an abrupt halt any cavalry attack and force infantrymen to be funneled into open spaces, where guns could be brought to bear on them. A deep and wide dry ditch fronted the redoubts as well, which would force any troops somehow successfully making their way to the main line to scale the steep slope of the fortification before gaining entry. The Yankees did not know it at the time, but the Confederates had also buried groups of mines in places,

which would wreak deadly havoc on any enemy force attempting to advance across the field.[17]

Confederates were still busily laboring to improve their position and would do so up the very moments before the climactic assault on April 9. Some of the hundreds of slave laborers utilized in the construction of the network of defenses around Mobile were apparently still present behind the lines at Blakeley as the siege commenced, as dispatches during the siege reveal officials directing that squads of workmen fell additional timber at various spots. Rebel engineers were frantically trying to shore up their defenses, as evidenced by a message sent by an engineer to headquarters on April 7: "I wish you to have made by Lt. Garland's squad of engineer troops and any other rough carpenters you can get from Genl. Liddell a large number of cheveaux de frieze…to be used on right-left flank of Blakeley line."[18]

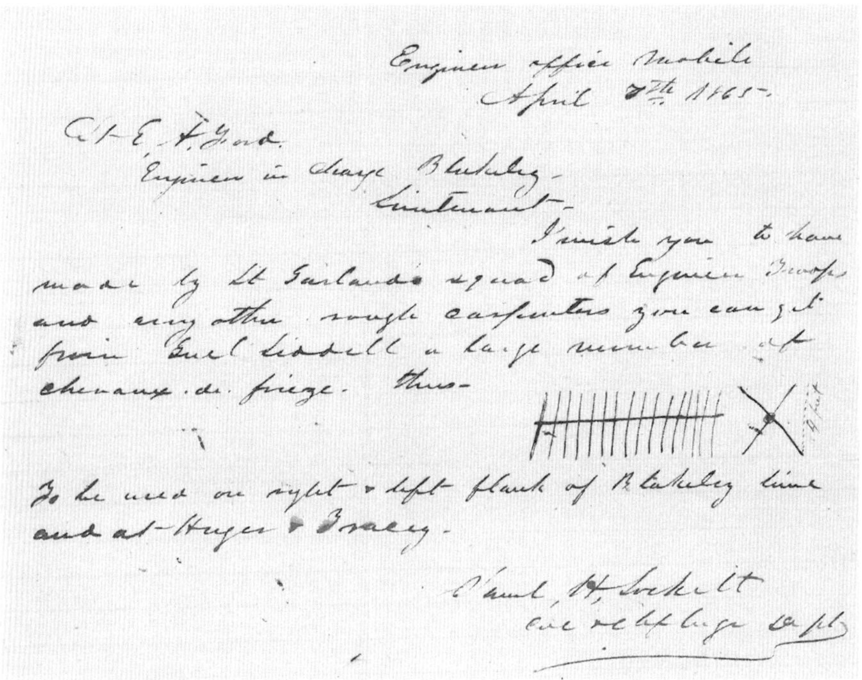
Engineer office Mobile
April 7th 1865.

Lt E. A. Ford.
Engineer in charge Blakeley.
Lieutenant—
I wish you to have made by Lt Garland's squad of Engineer Troops and any other rough carpenters you can get from Genl Liddell a large number of chevaux de frieze. thus—

To be used on right & left flank of Blakeley line and at Huger & Tracy.

Saml H. Lockett
Col & Chf Engr Dept

Letter from Chief Engineer Samuel Lockett to headquarters in Mobile, April 7, 1865. *Alabama Department of Archives and History.*

Behind all these defenses stood men on both extremes of the spectrum of experience in combat. About half had experienced intense fighting throughout the Civil War's Western Theater. Many were serving their fourth year in Confederate gray, having enlisted early in the war and endured siege and privation at Vicksburg, confronted one of the largest Federal armies to be put into the field in the west at several pitched battles in front of Atlanta and remained steady through bitter cold to fight overwhelming numbers on the frosty fields at Nashville. Steady, determined commanders such as General Francis M. Cockrell, a stalwart veteran with a broken finger he had purposely set in a way that allowed him a better grip on, among other things, his sword handle, and Colonel Elijah Gates, missing an arm lost after wounds in previous battles, commanded these rugged veterans. On the other hand, about half of the troops defending Blakeley were raw teenage conscripts and a sprinkling of men in their late forties or early fifties who had been too old for previous drafts and for whom the coming siege would be their first taste of combat. They were, as a group, untested in battle and highly suspect as a fighting force. While Confederate authorities expected a spirited defense of their position from the veteran units, they took pains to communicate how important it was that the inexperienced units understand they were to hold their position "to the last," "with the determination never to surrender."[19]

The Federals entrenched upon arrival to provide a measure of protection from the Confederate gunners, ultimately constructing three distinct lines of earthworks progressively closer to Fort Blakeley during the course of a nine-day siege. Each was a little more substantial than the last, defining the forward progress of the army as it moved "by gradual approaches with pick and shovel." A soldier of the Sixth Minnesota left a witty account of what life was like upon arrival in front of the fort prior to any protecting earthworks being constructed by the besiegers. Stopping in what is now known as Saluda Hill Cemetery, opposite the current park entrance on Highway 225 and about one thousand yards from the main lines of Fort Blakeley, he recorded that he found the grave of a Revolutionary soldier (Zachariah Godbold) among the interments. Setting up camp among the shady trees in the cemetery, he found the location to be discouragingly well within reach of the Rebel gunners. "On two or three occasions shells reached the brigade camp," he noted, "one of which cut off a thick pine near to Godbold's grave, but did not injure either living or dead."[20]

The Union troops would remember as a hallmark of their time at Blakeley the labor-intensive digging they performed to gain some measure of protection from enemy fire. The men performed the work gladly, though, even prior to the issuance of shovels, when all they had as tools were the bayonets and the tin plates in their haversacks, for it meant life or death. Soldiers "soon went down into the earth like moles," reported one Federal officer. "The laziest man that lives will work under circumstances like these." According to John Scott of the 32nd Iowa, "every man had his gun in one hand and spade in the other." The members of the besieging army learned in short order to labor nocturnally lest they become easy targets. "These trenches are always dug at night, no talking above a whisper being permitted, and no noise but that which comes from the pick and shovel," remembered one trooper.[21]

In front of the Yankee lines was a series of shallow rifle pits where advanced skirmishers were placed. These pits not only served as the location for small squads of sentinels but also became the beachhead from which additional lines could be formed. Major Ephraim Brown explained process in a letter home to his family: "[W]e threw up fortifications to protect our camp and that night following threw up rifle pits about 100 yards in front of our camps. On the next night we dug another pit 150 yds. in advance of the first. On the next evening we threw up another rifle pit still 150 yards in advance of the 2nd pit." Henry C. Merriam of the 73rd USCT left us with an even more detailed account of the process:

> *The usual way of locating advanced parallels was to send forward a line of skirmishers after dark to seize a position about one hundred yards in advance, more or less, according to topographical conditions, and when this line was assured in its position another line supplied with picks and shovels, was sent forward to join the first, when the line so established would intrench* [sic] *themselves as they stood. This done the occupants of these pits would extend them right and left to form a continuous line. Meanwhile saps or zig-zag approaches were also made to connect these parallels, so that officers and men could pass from one parallel to another in safety by night or day. These advances were made under the supervision of brigade commanders, who reported their progress daily to higher authority. This work was of course made as difficult and dangerous as possible by the besieged garrison, by means of frequent sallies, by night and day, and by means of fire-balls tossed into our lines from cohorn mortars and exposing our men to fire at short range while at their work.*[22]

The result of all the digging, in the homespun prose of one Iowa soldier, was that the Federals soon "were getting into neighborly closeness with the Johnnies." By the end of the siege, the battlefield at Fort Blakeley looked and felt more like the contested terrain of Europe in the cataclysm known as World War I than anything most of the soldiers there had conceived when they first entered service—a complicated network of opposing earthworks and a no-man's-landing standing between.[23]

Among the most ingenious methods used by the Confederates to slow the Union advance were "fire-balls." Specially made shells coated with calcium oxide (quicklime) ignited and fired into the air from mortars, they enabled the Rebels to briefly light up the field in front of them at night and expose the position of entrenching Federals with high, arcing shots delivering an eerie, flickering white glow. Similar in effect to large, brilliant Roman candles, fire-balls were a novel device utilizing what was actually rather widely available technology that had been adapted to military purposes in the latter stages of the war. General Liddell took pains to make sure such shells were created by his engineers, and he stated their purpose explicitly in a dispatch to subordinates: "The enemy are trying to advance their lines during the night, and I want to light up the front of our works, in order to see their dispositions and allow the artillery to be used with effect." On

Union lines at Blakeley today. *Historic Blakeley State Park.*

The remnants of a "zig-zag" approach trench on the battlefield at Blakeley. *Historic Blakeley State Park.*

April 8, Liddell ordered that "at 9 pm fire balls be thrown from Redoubts 1 and 4." We have very few descriptions of how and to what practical effect these devices were employed beyond such scant mentions, but it requires little imagination to envision in the mind's eye the way such ordnance might send besieging troops scurrying for cover as the defenders of the fort strained to see what the brief illumination revealed before them so that they could better aim their shots downrange.[24]

But the Confederates in Fort Blakeley did do all within their power to disrupt the progress of their adversary through more conventional means as well. They launched several sorties, or small-scale attacks, from their main lines to break up Union work crews under cover of night. Silently charging into the darkness at appointed times toward the sound of digging to within point-blank range of unsuspecting Yankees in advanced positions, squads of a few dozen to a few hundred Rebels on multiple occasions tried to make the bluecoats more hesitant in their work. At midnight one evening during the siege, for example, Captain John Murphy of the 58th Illinois recorded in his report of the operation that "the enemy made a sudden dash in considerable force, their old and new picket forming a heavy skirmish line, which was backed by a strong reserve." With an entire section of the line suddenly and unexpectedly under attack, the Federals were caught completely off guard and scrambled clumsily to make a defense. "The whispered orders of the officers could be distinctly heard in our pits," Murphy wrote, revealing just how close they had gotten before being discovered. The men of the 58th managed to cobble together a skirmish line of their own in moments despite the chaos, entering into a forty-five-minute firefight in which each man was estimated to have fired several dozen rounds.[25]

In another incident, recorded by a member of the 20th Iowa, Confederates launched a sortie a little past 3:00 a.m. along his section of the line. "They started up the other score, our regiment was run out to the reserve picket pit, they kept up the row for about half an hour, sending shells very close, but hurting no one." The attacks did not materially slow down the overall progress of the besieging army, but they did keep men on their toes and yielded many sleepless nights for the troops manning the advanced pits, as they strained to discern every noise they heard in their front at night lest they find a band of Rebels suddenly upon them. "The Johnnies seem determined to disturb our slumbers as much as possible," summarized a drowsy Lieutenant Colonel Hervey Craven of the 89th Indiana in a letter home after experiencing one of these sorties. The men managed to grow oddly acclimated to their situation though. Craven likely spoke for many when he recorded in his account of the progress of the siege how he had become "so accustomed to it that it don't disturb me much. In fact I begin to feel figidity when there is a lull in the discharge of artillery and musketry."[26]

Featuring the sniping of riflemen, coordinated small-scale infantry assaults and 'round-the-clock artillery bombardment, the siege of Fort Blakeley was a twenty-four-hour-long firefight for a solid week. Sharpshooters with little to do but watch for any movement along enemy lines blazed away at any target of opportunity that presented itself during the day, and artillery launched a variety of projectiles that made life along the front lines and well to the rear hazardous for men in both armies day and night. "I write amid the terrible thunder of artillery and the crash of musketry," read a typical letter home by an officer in the 122nd Illinois, "while I write the enemy are throwing shells in to our camp." Frederick Pell of the 76th Illinois recorded in his journal in simple terms how the Confederates "keep up a continuous fire day and night." "The Rebels shelled our camp this morning without mercy," another Federal from Iowa penned in a note to his family during the siege, while an Indiana trooper hurriedly recorded in his diary how his company had been "under fire all the time....Awful heavy cannonading. Tremendous bombing at the fort." The Yankee troopers gave as good as they got, despite having only about half of the number of artillery pieces on the field as their adversaries. On April 8, 1865, alone, one Union battery (Battery G, 2nd Illinois Light Artillery) sent more than two hundred rounds from its four twelve-pound Napoleons downrange toward the Rebel earthworks. The noise of all this activity rising from the battlefield could be heard across the waters of the delta in Mobile and throughout the bay region for miles, a steady low rumble becoming the soundtrack to the desperate struggle being waged along the Tensaw.[27]

While most of the fire described came from ordnance pieces along the Rebel line, some, especially early in the siege, were fired from Confederate gunboats in that venerable river and targeted the Federal right flank. The CSS *Nashville*, one of the largest ironclads built by the Confederacy, and the CSS *Morgan*, a sidewheel steamer that had taken part in the Battle of Mobile Bay, on several occasions did what they could to make life uncomfortable for the bluecoats before guns could be put into place to drive them off. Captain Joseph Fry, aboard the *Morgan* one afternoon, remembered how the Rebel sailors "had orders to shell their lines vigorously, and we did so up to dinner time." During the noonday break for a meal, however, as the crew was "quietly munching on our corn bread and sour bacon," the "whiz! bang!" of Federal shells from a masked battery that had gotten its range opened up a curious duel at the distance of about one thousand yards. After a little more than an hour into the exchange, the *Morgan* had taken several debilitating hits, including one dangerously near the waterline on its starboard side. Guns that could no longer be serviced due to lack of ammunition were moved to the port side of the vessel in an attempt to place the hole ripped open by a Federal Parrott round above water. Thus disabled, the captain at length ordered the boat back to Mobile.[28]

The ground-shaking power of the big guns and the carefully choreographed work of the gunners in their deadly mission was a sight to behold. Lieutenant George D. Carrington of the 11th Illinois left perhaps one of the best descriptions of the batteries in action:

> *After the gun was sighted by the Sergeant, gave it a jerk and a whang, with a whip-like crack. Keen as a squirrel rifle, only so much louder, was the report, while a cloud of white smoke rolled away from the muzzle. Every man about the place had his eyes upon the Rebel works expecting an answering shot. We could trace the course of the shot as with a soul harrowing swish and screech it struck the top of the timber beyond.... White smoke floating so gracefully away. The weave of the men, back and forth, as they sponged the piece, the black water flowing from the muzzle, the red flame as it sprang from the gun.... The man running from the limber chest to the gun with the charge. The man at the breech with the friction primer.... The quick movements of it all. The Lieutenant with glass watching the effects of each shot. It was a grand sight that war alone can produce.*[29]

All the constant artillery and small-arms fire rendered deadly wounds and death sudden and unpredictable daily realities, and narrow escapes a routine occurrence. Artillery and mortar fire rained death on the unwary, killing men at their posts and in their tents at random, while accurate fire from Rebel skirmishers made constant vigilance a must at the front. "Each day they would kill or wound some one in almost every regiment," observed Major Ephraim Brown of the 114th Ohio in a letter home. James M. Dunn recorded in his diary how the bombardment proved dismayingly indiscriminate, as he knew of a member of the Ambulance Corps far in the rear to have been struck down by a shell during the siege and witnessed an adjutant take a bullet in the mouth along the besieger's trench line. Colonel William T. Spicely recalled how during a single day on the front "five bullets cut the sod above the loop hole through which we were shooting," but he coolly added, "We escaped their deadly message." Confederates faced many of the same dangers, especially as the Federals got within range of skilled sharpshooters and accurate artillery fire made life anywhere out of the bombproofs hazardous. In a telling admission of the proximity to which they had advanced and the firepower they were able to bring to bear, General Liddell did what he could to secure more sharpshooters in gray to counter the brazen Yankees, who "kill and wound men at the Blakely Wharf" more than half a mile from the main Union line.[30]

For those on the front lines, the danger was especially present and continual, but they learned to adapt to their situation and even find in it some occasional humor. When they saw the tell-tale smoke of fire from the Confederate artillery, almost before the report met their ears the men were shouting "to your holes, here she comes!" One man reflected that they did not have to be warned twice. "The weather was fine, our rations ample and we slept in our bomb-proofs when we did sleep, out of the reach of the big shells (our men called them camp kettles), which the rebel gunboats tossed over to us," remembered Charles S. Hills in a postwar reflection. Jonathan Merriam of the 117th Illinois was one of several to recall humorous incidents, such as "when a cannonball comes close over the reserve post, the way the boys hunt their holes is a caution, sometimes when in a hurry, they go in head foremost like a frog into the water....I sometimes could not help laughing, if it cost my life....It is surprising to see how flat men can lay on the ground, when a Minnie Ball comes whistling over." Once it became obvious that Confederate gunners were using flickering campfires that they could see in the distance as targets, Lieutenant Colonel James F. Drish of the 122nd Illinois wrote of how "you would have laughed to see the boys put them out." Some even used the constant danger they faced as the context for practical jokes. Charles Boyd, a sergeant in the 46th Illinois, amused himself one day by throwing clay balls at the tree his lieutenant was hiding behind as he tried to observe the Confederates. Thinking that he had been spotted by sharpshooters, the officer dodged the phantom rifleman furiously until he discovered the ruse. "We used to laugh over it afterward," he would record in a history of the regiment he penned later, "but at the time the lieutenant couldn't see the joke."[31]

The weather during the siege of Blakeley featured warm spring days and cool nights with occasional light showers, an altogether rather pleasant stretch compared to the area's damp and sometimes frigid winters and its sweltering humid summers. As might be expected among a large group of men living in the elements, however, encounters with the natural environment were not uniformly pleasant. One member of the 11th Wisconsin had a particularly bad experience with poison sumac, for example. A short time after encountering the plant, he wrote home in misery that "my face is swelling up hugely & my hands and arms are breaking out also other parts." The next day, he reported his deteriorating condition to be very painful and worsening. "My eyes are swelled shut. I can scarcely move my hands, arms and legs are awful. The Doctor gives me a wash of sugar and lead but it does no good & I can get no relief." How many of his compatriots suffered similar maladies is unknown, but with snakes, poison plants, mosquitoes, ticks and a wide variety of other irritants and nuisances present in the natural environment, it can well be imagined that a portion of the otherwise healthy men on the field at Blakeley were inconvenienced to a great degree during the siege.[32]

More serious maladies stalked the men at Blakeley, as they did in army camps throughout the war. Through a combination of poor sanitation, primitive medical conditions, poor food served irregularly and the stress of life in the field in battle conditions, men could become afflicted with a devil's panoply of afflictions that could at best sideline them for short periods or, in severe cases, take their life. "I have been quite less well in my bowels for a week caused I think by hard living," wrote Lieutenant Colonel James F. Drish of the 122nd Illinois in a letter that succinctly summed up the experience of a wide portion of his army in a few phrases. "How do you suppose it goes with us down here with nothing to eat and eating that little and sleeping under the fire of the enemies guns. Laying down at night not knowing you may find a Rebel shell in bed with you before morning....It is not an infrequent occurrence that officers and men have been killed since the siege of Mobile commenced while sitting or sleeping in their tents." One man of the 76th Illinois wrote home of what the army was enduring in even plainer language. "We are having a hard time." And so they did as the siege progressed, blue and gray, black and white.[33]

In such conditions, men looked forward to whatever diversions presented themselves. Soldiers eagerly anticipated the delivery of mail in camp, straining for an opportunity to hear from home even to the point of waiting under fire to see if a missive with their name on the cover had arrived. "Yesterday evening," wrote one Federal, "the mail came into camp....The Captain was standing under a friendly pine tree calling over the names on the letters...the usual crowd was around him and every shell that would come you should see the crowd dodge and scatter, but still it did not decrease the desire to hear from home." As might be imagined, this correspondence was typically filled with updates on home and health, well wishes and hopes for a safe return. It gave them a reminder of what they were fighting for and, for most, something to look forward to. Not all of the news contained in this coveted correspondence was good, however. In his diary, one Illinois trooper recorded that on April 5 he "got a letter today that my wife is laying at the point of death." The entry is a poignant reminder that many of the men behind the earthworks had much besides the enemy on their mind on occasion. As in every other circumstance, life went on.[34]

When not on the front lines on duty, the men spent long, dull hours in camp passing the time as best they could. Many hours were consumed in conversation with their fellow troops or in writing letters home, both commonly studded with commentary on their current circumstances and their hopes to soon improve them. Some played games to while away the time, ranging from cards to baseball. The latter sport was popular especially among soldiers in the Union army during the war, and much of its popularity in postwar America can be traced to the spread of knowledge of the game in military camps such as those at Blakeley. John Thomas of the 47th Indiana recorded that in the nice spring weather, his unit "had a good game of ball" behind the lines, but he gave no description of what sort of equipment they used or rules they abided by. Some men tried their hand at fishing in the many small creeks and streams coursing through the ravines of Blakeley as they made their way toward the Tensaw River, apparently with little luck. At least a few took note of the unique natural environment they found on the Gulf Coast, the campaign being the first time many had seen such foreign sights as sandy beaches and longleaf pine forests. One man of the 27th Iowa marveled at the site of "a curiosity called Venus fly trap."[35]

The occasional care package that arrived in the camps broke the monotony and danger of life on the front, however briefly, and reminded soldiers of the loved ones and home life for which they ultimately believed they were fighting. As a gesture of their support, the ladies of Mobile sent some care packages of goodies to the soldiers in the trenches at Blakeley during the siege, filled with delights in short supply such as fresh clothing, coffee, sugar, bread, cakes and other items. Within the Federal camps, army mail delivered infrequent but cherished treats along with letters from loved ones far away. Thomas Fisher of the 11th Illinois, for example, excitedly recorded in his diary that on Saturday, April 8, his brother had received some pickles, an occurrence superseded only by the regiment's receipt of a rare issuance of a ration of tobacco the same afternoon—taken together, a banner day for the Fishers. In truth, tobacco, among the most sought-after of government provisions for Federal troops, was cause for celebration any time it became

Union soldiers playing a game of baseball at a prison in North Carolina, 1863. *Library of Congress.*

available, whatever the source. "Tobacco is dear stuff down here," observed one Wisconsin soldier, who went on to note that a financial market for the product had developed in camp that made it among the most valuable of commodities in informal camp exchange.[36]

Desire for the leaf actually contributed to some unauthorized fraternization between enemy pickets along portions of the lines at Blakeley. In the last days of the siege, "the opposing rifle pits and our outer parallels were no more than eighty yards apart," remembered Charles S. Hills of the 10th Kansas. This proximity "led to quiet little truces, when the muskets would be left in the trenches and the blue and grey meet each other socially, half way, to swap lies for ten minutes, and at other times trade coffee for a Mobile paper and a plug of tobacco. When the truce was ended and both sides started back to their works, the Rebs would call out: 'Say, Yanks, if you all git in first, don't shoot till we uns git in.' Nor did they; but woe to the head that showed itself a half minute later." Officers did the best they could to discourage the disorderly practice, of course.[37]

With the help of those newspapers, letters from home and rumors of developments passed along in camp, soldiers tried to keep up with the progress of the war as best they could. All of these sources of information were filled with perhaps as much speculation as verified fact. It became something of a hobby for the men in the trenches to extrapolate from the little bits of information peppered with heavy doses of conjecture they received their own predictions on what course the war might actually be taking. Rumors ran rampant at Blakeley that Southern cities elsewhere were falling or even had fallen into Union hands, that General Lee and General Joseph E. Johnston's armies had been cornered and captured and that the Confederacy had collapsed. Some in both blue and gray dismissed it all as a cruel hoax, discounting the reports of a nearing end to the conflict as idle fantasy and instead choosing to focus their efforts on steeling themselves for a continued long and bitter fight. Regardless of what may or may not be happening elsewhere, the fact that they faced a deadly situation where they were forced the men to focus on the present. Unsure what to make of all the rumors floating on the spring air in south Alabama, one Yankee wrote in a letter to family on the eve of the battle for Fort Blakeley that no matter what was occurring elsewhere, "we have a nasty job here. It's a worse place to take than Vicksburg."[38]

Many shared such resolve. The majority of the men at Blakeley, in both blue and gray, had fought multiple years in a war that had been filled with all manner of spectacular predictions and inaccurate prognostication. They had learned through hard campaigning and constant exposure to the dangers of combat to focus on the task at hand. To the modern reader, it might seem easier to comprehend how the soldiers in the ranks of the Federal army could maintain such a determination to see their task through, for in hindsight we know the Southern cause by this point in the war to have been hopelessly doomed and victory must have seemed within their grasp. Yet the Rebels, no less aware of the reverses Confederate arms had suffered over the previous years, persisted remarkably despite the mounting evidence of the dissolution of the nation for which they were fighting. Men in both armies were still prepared to put their lives on the line despite what they knew about the progress of the war, as it was by no means as clear to them as we sometimes try to make it appear today that the war was at an end. That they did so reveals less their collective naïveté than our contemporary shallow understanding of the strength of their concepts of honor, duty and conviction, as well as the power contained in the bonds of camaraderie derived from shared experience.

During the course of the siege, a reporter from a Mobile paper wrote about his visit to the Confederate lines at Fort Blakeley. The description of the morale displayed by the troops he provided, while certainly in part a form of editorial bravado meant to instill confidence in readers or shame those who had wavered in their belief in the Southern cause, demonstrates the in-the-moment reality of life in a war zone:

> *The excitement attendant on being under fire, and the fearlessness of the troops, is inspiring and exhilarating. This morning the firing along the line was quite heavy, and successful to our arms....I would like to transport over to Blakeley a lot of our Royal Street croakers, and let them mingle with the troops. They would first become ashamed of themselves, and then pluck up a little courage, and, in all probability, form a first rate opinion about our success and the value of Confederate money, even if they should still continue to croak and grind out the highest price for their wares. The courage, pluck, and spirit of the troops is as good as the most sanguine could desire. Where all behave so well and so much confidence exists, non-combatants should not doubt. Let our brave boys be well fed and provided with all things needed for their comfort, and all will go well.*[39]

A week into the siege of Fort Blakeley, clear progress had been made in advancing toward the Rebel position by the Federal army. At that pace, however, they realized that it might be several more days before Union gunners could suppress fire from the garrison the way their compatriots had done at Spanish Fort. There, an even greater disparity of numbers let them move their lines up to point-blank range, where a short, final rush was all that was needed to break Confederate lines. That is exactly what happened there on the evening of Saturday, April 8, but closing darkness had prevented the troops who had created the breach from fully understanding what they had done, and the garrison's commander, Brigadier General Gibson, had skillfully evacuated his post with virtually his entire army overnight rather than face certain defeat and capture in the morning. As news trickled in of what had occurred at Spanish Fort on the morning of April 9, Federal officers at Blakeley began to have serious concerns that the prey they had stalked for so long and at such high cost might attempt to give them the slip as well. The movement of transport vessels to and from the Blakeley dock, where they came to pick up a few evacuees from Spanish Fort who had made their way through the swamp during the night, only heightened fears that Fort Blakeley might be summarily abandoned. By midmorning, plans for an immediate assault were underway. As the Union artillery began shelling the Confederate lines as usual that morning, orders went out "to transfer to the Blakeley lines as rapidly as possible the siege guns (28) and mortars (16) that would be required if the place resisted an assault." Canby made a quick surveillance of the situation and found his men in good position to carry the Rebel works, noting in his after-action report that he had found "that the prospects of a successful assault were promising. The colored division had

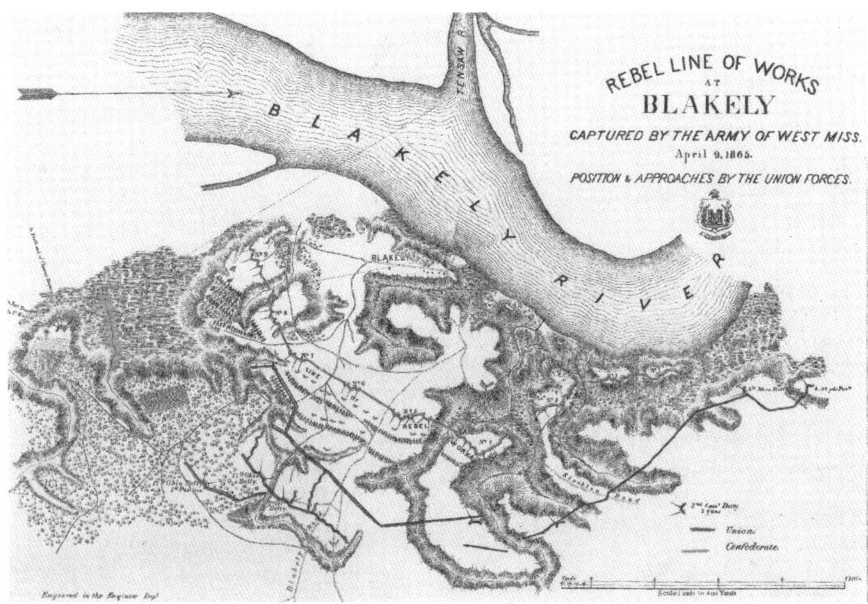

Positions of the Confederate and Union lines at Blakeley, April 1–9, 1865. *Library of Congress.*

already gained and held some important advantages on its front; Andrews' and Veatch's divisions were well up with their work, and the resistance of the enemy was less spirited than on previous days." By late afternoon, all arrangements had been made, and the troops were in position across a nearly four-mile arcing line mirroring that of the Confederates.[40]

The appointed time for the assault was 5:30 p.m., but as the Union lines stretched so far over varying terrain and some regiments had a portion of their forces in advanced rifle pits and others in reserve, not everyone got into position at the exact same moment. Some stood in readiness for more than half an hour, while others received their orders at the last minute and rushed to their posts from routine camp duties. The actual assault seems to have gotten underway just a few minutes after the appointed time, as a great many of the after-action reports by officers indicate the approximate time of the assault to be closer to 5:45 p.m. But in truth, it did not begin promptly at the exact same moment across the length of the Federal line. Once lead elements of the besieging army got into motion in each sector, units on either side stepped out of the trenches moments later and began to run toward the Confederate lines as well. Whatever the exact time each regiment stepped onto the field, all were in motion by a quarter to 6:00 p.m., a massive blue wave of some sixteen thousand blue-clad troops in a thick, undulating line snaking across the landscape as a cacophony of small-arms fire, shell bursts, cheering and yelling raged. Flags fluttered and waved across the landscape, above the whole panoply a thick column of smoke gradually enveloping the entire battlefield. The charge was one of the great spectacles of the Civil War.[41]

"After firing all day yesterday, the order came at 5 o'clock to cease firing," remembered one Federal artilleryman. "We began to wonder what was up. Soon we heard a yell and increased firing by the rebs. We looked over the works and our entire line from right to left was charging the reb works." With his battery falling silent so as to avoid endangering his own men as the charge got underway, he got a chance to observe the scene from a vantage point from which he could see a large swath of the battle line to the north and south. "We had a good view. It was a glorious sight, a line of 15,000 men marching steady into the jaws of death."[42]

Following is the story of those frantic moments of the late afternoon of Sunday, April 9, 1865, presented sector by sector as told by the men who fought the Battle of Fort Blakeley.

Chapter 2

The Battle of Fort Blakeley

The Fight at Redoubts 3 and 4

Redoubts 3 and 4 were the scenes of some of the most intense fighting of the Battle of Fort Blakeley. Among the more substantial of the nine major fortified positions along the Confederate line, they were manned by some of the most veteran troops of the garrison. The fortifications stand just a few hundred yards distant from each other on opposite sides of a wide ravine through which flows a small stream, today largely overtaken by a beaver pond. Redoubt 3 lies just to the northwest of Redoubt 4, nearer the river, and demarcates the area where the Confederate line angles sharply away from the Tensaw to make its broad arc along the central part of the line. While Redoubt 5 could be seen to the immediate right (south) of Redoubt 4, Redoubt 3 stood almost directly behind that fortification.

The area of Redoubts 3 and 4, accessed via the park's Battlefield Road, is the most prominent part of the battlefield at Blakeley and is the focal point of some of the park's efforts to interpret the battle. The relatively open field between Redoubt 4 and the Union lines some four hundred yards distant, today in the process of restoration as a longleaf pine habitat, is the only place where large sections of the earthworks of the contending armies are easily visible from one location, making it the perfect spot for reenactments and living history demonstrations. It is still referred to informally as "the Battlefield" in park literature, even though the entirety of the property is, in truth, the site of the battle; the area in front of Redoubt 4, in actuality, occupies only about one-tenth of its acreage. The park's northern border

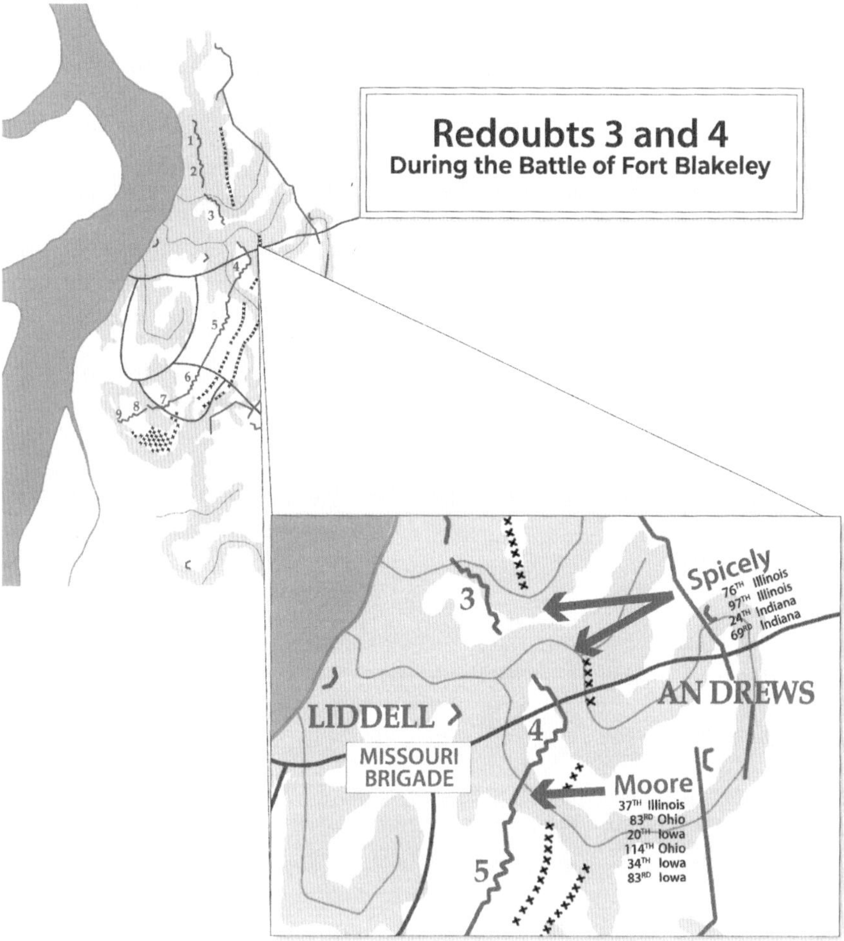

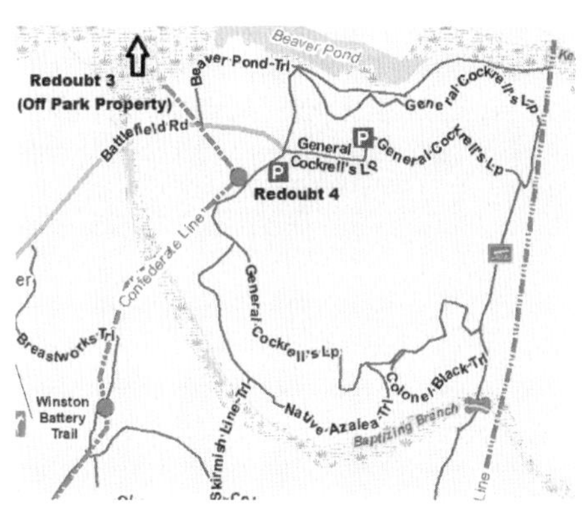

Above: Redoubts 3 and 4 during the Battle of Fort Blakeley. *Historic Blakeley State Park.*

Left: Area of Redoubts 3 and 4 today as depicted on park visitor map. *Historic Blakeley State Park.*

runs between the fortifications, with Redoubt 3 located just off its property (and therefore not currently accessible for tours) but in a remarkable state of preservation.

Redoubt 4 is the only portion of the Confederate line at Blakeley that has been reconstructed to any degree. The position was once among the most easily accessed portions of the battlefield prior to the land coming under the control of the state park in the 1990s and, therefore, was heavily looted by relic hunters. The first professional archaeological survey of the earthwork, conducted in late 1970s, described this particular redoubt as thoroughly pock-marked by holes and so reduced in size that its original shape and scale were barely recognizable. Further, it was declared "totally devoid of artifactural remains" at the time of the study. Beginning in the 1980s, after the establishment of the park as a state entity in 1981, reenactors shored up its sagging walls with creosoted timber, added dirt to its diminished ramparts and eroded floor to approximate their original height and reconstructed some of the interior features of the position to serve as a unique exhibit on the form and function of the Rebel fortifications. In recent years, park staff members have continued this work by clearing trees that had been allowed to grow on the fortification's walls and by placing a series of reconstructions of the obstacles to enemy approach that stood in front of Redoubt 4 at the time of the battle: sharpened stakes, *cheveaux de frise* and rows of abatis. The numerous stumps in front of the position remind visitors that in places the Confederates had strung telegraph wire between stumps of trees felled to create fields of fire as an additional impediment to advance against them on foot or on horseback. On the opposite side of the clearing from Redoubt 4 is the third parallel of Union trenches, a distinct low earthen wall fronted by a row of shallow rifle pits. In front of the hulking remains of the gun emplacement erected by the 15th Massachusetts Battery during the siege lies a unique serpentine excavation known as a "zig-zag." An approach trench dug under fire or under the cover of night, this extraordinarily rare battlefield feature reveals how the besieging army advanced from one parallel to another. By snaking their way out of the main line to a new position rather than moving straight ahead, skirmishers were better protected from enemy fire in their direction should their work be discovered.[43]

Typical of the rolling terrain that predominates throughout the landscape at Blakeley, the land in front of Redoubts 3 and 4 features swells and slopes of varying scale. On the extreme right in front of Redoubt 4 stretches a narrow strip of table-flat land that, further to the right, drops off into another small but steep ravine. Directly in front of the position, the plain is interrupted by

Brigadier General Francis M. Cockrell. *Alabama Department of Archives and History.*

a gently sloping draw through which Battlefield Road runs. To the left, the terrain drops off toward the aforementioned beaver pond and then rises again to the high ground on which Redoubt 3 sits. To its left, a shallow dip defines the space between it and Redoubt 2. It would be through this bucolic landscape that in the late afternoon of April 9 hardy midwestern units hailing from Iowa, Illinois, Indiana and Ohio would advance in a headlong charge against a murderous fire toward the stalwart veterans of the Missouri Brigade and one of the heaviest concentrations of artillery on the battlefield.

Standing at the interpretive panels at the front left of Redoubt 4 and looking down Battlefield Road to where it terminates in front of the Federal rifle pits, one can see where the charge began in this sector and perhaps best understand the hazardous nature of the assault. With a cheer, the Yankee column leaped from the trenches in the distance at about 5:45 p.m. and headed toward the Confederate line at a run. The skirmish line, occupying the rifle pits in front of the main trenches, formed the vanguard. The men were soon joined by a heavier main line. As they made their way toward

Redoubt 4, the attackers would have been visible for a considerable distance, an undulating wave of blue-clad troops crested by the flinty steel glinting of bayonets. An array of national and regimental flags waved crazily at the fore of each advancing group in a gaudy display of color.[44]

The attackers had barely emerged from their trenches when puffs of black smoke and earth could be seen shooting upward in isolated places where the very ground appeared to rupture; portions of the Union force had stepped right into fields strewn with landmines. The deadly havoc these devices wrought on those unfortunate enough to have tripped them—severing legs and arms from bodies and ripping through flesh and bone with brutal suddenness—brought home the deadly nature of the endeavor within seconds. In an instant, the full weight of Rebel ordnance was directed at the attackers, as hundreds of rifles sent heavy lead bullets whizzing downrange, and artillery of a variety of calibers launched into action with deafening bellows as flame leaped from their muzzles and hundreds of pounds of grape, canister and shell were sent howling into the mass of humanity. A heavy cloud of sulfurous smoke from the discharge of weaponry soon hung heavy in the spring air, seemingly hastening dusk in the late afternoon. In full view of Confederate gunners, the Federal column nonetheless steadily advanced into the heart of what one soldier described poetically as an "awful hissing seething roaring fire of flame," slowed only temporarily by the variety of obstructions placed by Confederates designed to arrest their advance. Rebels in the rifle pits in front of the main line, having fired a few ragged volleys at the attackers, began leaving their positions in small groups and running pell-mell back toward the redoubt as the Yankee wave neared within minutes. It was all a grand sight to behold and a scene that became seared into the memories of the participants who survived the brief but intense fight. "When that line was moving up, I lived years," Corporal W.H. Hart of the 2nd Connecticut light artillery, who observed the charge from his battery position, would remember. Confederates would recall the scene in awe as well. Attempting to describe what he had witnessed in his diary later, Corporal William H. Kavanaugh of the 2nd and 6th Missouri, said simply that "[a]n imposing sight, truly, was this, and one never to be forgotten." Capturing the essence of the scene in powerful metaphor, Lieutenant Colonel Charles Black of the 37th Illinois remembered how, once the guns opened, "the thunder and lightning of battle rose above."[45]

Despite the particularly stout resistance and stubborn nature of the defense the combat-hardened Confederates in this sector of the battlefield put up, sheer numbers overwhelmed the fort's defenders in less than half

The Battle of Fort Blakeley by Rick Reeves. This depiction of the Battle of Fort Blakeley was authorized by the Baldwin County Commission as part of the three-year commemoration of Alabama's Bicentennial, 2017–19. It shows the Union charge of April 9, 1865, as viewed from the vantage point of the parapet of Redoubt 4, looking southeast. *Baldwin County Commission.*

an hour. Quickly taking possession of the trenches between Redoubts 3 and 4, attackers swept up the ravine to a position virtually behind the latter fortification, briefly bringing the garrison here under attack from front, side and back. Intense, close-quarters firefights raged on and within the parapets, and at least two color-bearers were killed in attempting to plant their flags on the Confederate works. The final shots fired in this sector of the battlefield were between the Federals who had taken control of Redoubt 4 and a small group of resolute Missourians who had attempted to form a short second line in the brush to its rear. Regrouping and advancing on this position, the Yankees soon captured all those who had not broken and ran toward the river, including General Francis M. Cockrell.

Today, Redoubt 4, the approximate center of the Confederate line and the northernmost section of the fort accessible for touring, is where the story of the Battle of Fort Blakeley is most often communicated to park guests. Some half a dozen interpretive panels dot the area, explaining strategy and tactics and communicating how the battle unfolded both on the spot and in general. It features prominently in the park's self-guided battlefield tour

Regimental flag of the 47th Indiana Infantry. *Indiana War Memorial.*

as well, serving as the spot for the most thorough demonstration of how the fight unfolded. It is significant to note that of the thirteen Medals of Honor awarded for action in the battle, four citations would involve this individual sector of the battlefield: First Lieutenant Thomas H.L. Payne, 37th Illinois, for leading a company that had no commissioned officers present; Captain Patrick H. Pentzer, 97th Illinois, for being among the first to enter Confederate lines at Redoubt 4, receiving the surrender of General Cockrell and capturing his headquarters flag; First Sergeant Joseph Stickels, 83rd Ohio, for capturing a flag of the Missouri Brigade in Redoubt 4; and Lieutenant Colonel Victor Vifquain, 97th Illinois, for capturing a flag of the Missouri Brigade between Redoubts 3 and 4.[46]

In Their Own Words

Union Lines

2nd Division, XIII Corps
Andrews's Division

Brigadier General Christopher C. Andrews
"[I]t was a quarter to six when the movement commenced.…Instantly they were greeted with a shower of bullets, and before they had got twenty yards a few men fell…the Confederates were getting out of their rifle-pits and falling back to their main works in literal swarms.…Lieut. Wm. F. Kenaga [76th Illinois] was shot through a leg at the second abatis, and nearer the works was hit in the ankle-joint of his other leg; then, unable to walk, he kept upright on his knees and rallied and cheered the men. The color-sergeant, Hussey, was killed within twenty feet of the works; then the colors were taken by the noble and brave Corporal Goldwood, who, as he was planting them on the parapet, received the contents of three muskets so close that the discharge burnt his clothes, and he fell dead inside the works with the colors in his arms. Col. Busey ran along close the parapet, and, with his revolver, disabled the gunner of a howitzer about to be fired.…The colors of the regiment (97th Illinois) were planted on the works between the Stockton Road and the redoubt south of it, almost simultaneously with the 83rd Ohio.…Sergeant Edwin D. Lowe…planted them firmly on the works, then fell with a mortal wound. But the hand that struck him down was soon itself laid cold, by an unerring shot from one of the color-guard…

The infantry troops that manned [Redoubt 4]…stood up in a bold manner as if they hoped to repulse them. There seemed to be a constant blaze of musketry along the breastworks. The artillery was served with the same desperate energy. The guns vomited forth grape and canister with a fury that made one shudder. But most of the shots went over the mark.… Lt.-Col. Baldwin was soon over the parapet; and seeing that the most of his regiment (83rd Ohio) was ready to mount the works, he jumped down inside, and cried out, 'Surrender!' The commanding officer inquired, 'To whom do we surrender?' Baldwin answered, 'To the 83rd Ohio.' Then the officer said, 'I believe we did that once before,' referring to a somewhat similar occasion at Vicksburg. It was about twenty minutes from the time the 83rd began the charge till it was in possession of the works; but some contest was kept up for a few minutes in rear of the redoubt after the first had entered.[47]

Above: Headquarters flag, 2nd Division, XIII Corps. *Illinois State Military Museum, Springfield.*

Left: Brigadier General Christopher C. Andrews. *Library of Congress.*

Redoubt 4 as it appeared in 1866, sketched on a return visit to the battlefield by Brigadier General Christopher C. Andrews. *From* The Campaign of Mobile.

The scene was picturesque and grand. From different points of view the assaulting lines could be seen for a mile or two....The regimental colors, though not in perfect line, were steadily advancing, and the troops were dashing on over and through the obstructions like a stormy wave...[48]

A man named Walker...had told his comrades where he would fall, and after they had passed the spot they looked back, and saw that he was indeed lying there."[49]

Moore's Brigade

20th Iowa Volunteer Infantry

The 20th Iowa had been attached to the Army of the Frontier prior to being assigned to the Department of Tennessee and then the Department of the Gulf. It participated in Schofield's campaign in southwest Missouri in the fall of 1862 and the Battle of Prairie Grove in December of that year. The 20th took part in the Vicksburg campaign, moving from there to service in Louisiana and Texas until being sent from New Orleans as part of the forces that laid siege to Fort Morgan in August 1864. It advanced on Fort Blakeley from Pensacola under General Steele. After the battle, it was mustered out of service at Mobile in July 1865.[50]

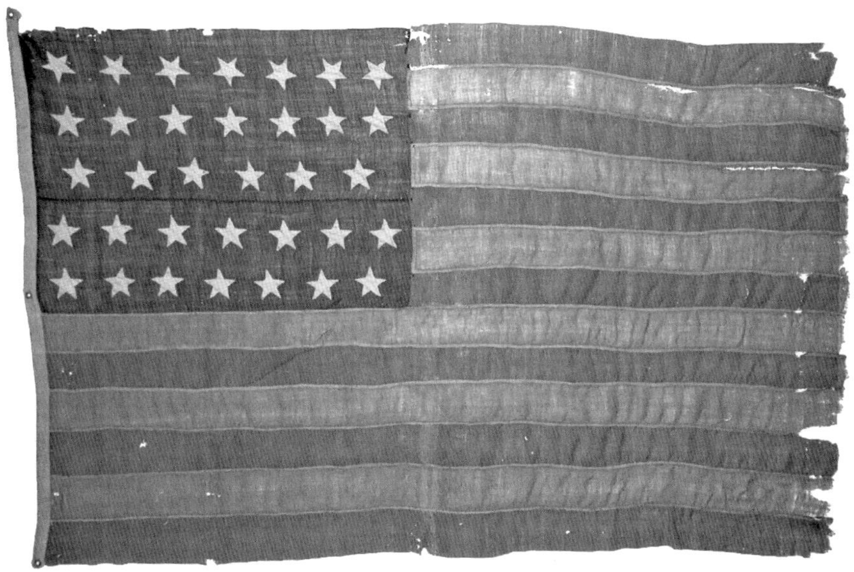

National flag carried by the 20th Iowa. *State Historical Museum of Iowa, Des Moines.*

Private Samuel Crawford

"[A]t 3 minutes before 5 o'clock the skirmishers started out of the reserve pit. About 15 minutes afterward the remainder of the line started within 45 minutes from that time we were in possession of the whole Rebel works with all their ammunition and ordinance [*sic*] and rations. We marched through to the river, visiting the commissary. The products were ham, hard tack, soap and tobacco....We got back into camp about 9 o'clock, had roll call, and hot coffee."[51]

37TH ILLINOIS INFANTRY REGIMENT

Organized in the summer of 1861, the 37th Illinois was originally known as the "Fremont Rifles." It first served as a part of the Army of the Frontier under Generals Curtis and Herron and participated in the Battle of Pea Ridge in March 1862. It guarded southwest Missouri afterward until being sent in pursuit of scattered Rebel forces in Arkansas that fall, during which its rapid marching earned it the nickname of the "Illinois Greyhounds." The 37th fought in the Battle of Prairie Grove in December 1862 and in the Battle of Chalk Bluffs in May 1863 prior to being sent to assist in the siege of Vicksburg, Mississippi. It saw service in Louisiana and Texas after that city's fall before being sent to Pensacola to join General Steele's 13th Army Corps

Above: National flag carried by the 37th Illinois Infantry. *Illinois State Military Museum, Springfield.*

Right: Lieutenant Colonel John Charles Black. *Library of Congress.*

in early 1865. After the capture of Fort Blakeley, the regiment was briefly stationed in Texas, where it was mustered out of service in May 1866.[52]

Brigadier General Eugene Payne

"We fell in and in less than five minutes our line was formed behind our advanced line of works. A large line of skirmishers were immediately deployed in front of us. Everything betokened work and all were convinced that an assault upon the enemy's works was intended immediately…at 20 minutes past five…the signal was given for them to advance, the men bounded from the works with a cheer, which sounded like the signal note of victory.…Steadily, gallantly they advanced; nine hundred yards of ground was to be passed over ere the enemy's works could be reached; yet not a man faltered, but right over they moved in the face of an awful fire, sending up cheer on cheer…into the midst of that awful hissing seething roaring fire of flame.…Every step we made was marked by a howling storm of shells and balls which fell like hail stones all about us straight across that nine hundred yards of abatis wire fence and torpedoes without a halt or a check straight after their glorious banner which color sergeant Grace dashed ahead with striving to be the first to plant it on their works did we move on until with a cheer which must have chilled the heart of every traitor there. We dashed up the sloping sides of the earthworks and rallied round our colors conquerors of all within."[53]

Lieutenant Colonel John Charles Black

"How they shelled us and how bullets sung their zooming song about our ears. How fragments struck all around us and how on one particular evening for half an hour the enemy paid us terrible compliments.…Sometimes when men anticipate an easy and perhaps bloodless exploit they respond to bugle call and drumbeat with noisy cheers and empty boastings. Not so on this occasion. Quickly they formed in line silently and with nervous tread they refiled from their camps.…The day was Sunday sunny clear and soft. The direction of our charge took us westward. Happy omen for these men of war who owe allegiance to that Land of Setting Sun. At 5:35 PM the skirmishers rose and passed rapidly over…to within 200 yards of the fort. Here they halted covered and commenced fire. Then at 5:45 the word 'forward' was given. I was in front of the center of the regt. and springing to the top of the parapet cast one glance around. For a mile on either side the earth seemed giving birth to men as they leaped up from the works and cheering shouting raging swept on like in color force and effect to a blue ocean wave. Instantly the enemy's works blazed with all wars fire. The thunder and the lightning of battle rose above....The whiz, whiz, of the minies. The scream and roar of shell and the deadly sickening swoosh of canister and grape.... From thousands of polished muskets the setting sun shone in bright star like reflections...the encanopying smoke hung heavier. Fifteen minutes passed in the breathless charge and battle noises were hushed while wild cries of triumph rung over the conquered wall. The rag was down and the last rays of the sun shone full on Old Glory waving over Blakeley Batteries. Oh, the life, the joy, the madness of that hour. Men shouted sung and cheered. They laughed and whooped and hugged each other, stern veterans who a short time before had parted not expecting again to meet oer the whither shore."[54]

Private T.J. Stow

"The skirmishers advanced and when half the distance intervened between them and the rebel works the order for a simultaneous advance was received, when the whole line advanced at the double quick over the brush and logs in abundance which obstructed our passage and added to this great inconvenience under which we labored....Three shells passed the whole length of our regiment, passing just in front of the colors, but still onward we pressed, our battle cry being victory or death. We passed over the rebel works with a tremendous yell. You would have thought if you had been there that all the fiends in human shape had broken loose from the lower regions and like an angel of light from Hell were on the point of visiting death and destruction to the southern chivalry in the last ditch. There were many hand to hand engagements occurred and privates used their bayonets or clubbed their muskets, but in less than one half hour after the charge commenced the fort and all was ours. We then marched down to the levee where we helped ourselves to tobacco, meal, crackers, meat, molasses, and whiskey....Boyd was shot thru the neck, causing instant death. He fell like a brave soldier at the enemy's rifle pit and his face to the foe."[55]

First Lieutenant Thomas H.L. Payne

"We had to climb over lines of brush and trees piled very high and then across a wide, deep, dry moat, filled with brush, before we could get a foothold on the works. All the ground over which we charged was covered with hidden torpedoes, making it doubly dangerous. I struck out for a corner of the earthworks, shouting, 'this way, company B!' and luckily found a place where a fallen tree formed a foot-bridge across the moat. I crossed upon this and a few of my company followed. In a minute I found myself inside the works within a few feet of a number of Confederate gunners."[56]

National flag carried by the 114th Ohio Infantry. *State of Ohio Adjutant General's Battle Flag Collection.*

114TH OHIO INFANTRY

The 114th Ohio mustered into service in September 1862 and saw action in the Yazoo Expedition and operations along the Mississippi before taking part in the Vicksburg campaign. It served in the Red River campaign afterward, before being sent to Pensacola in January 1865. After the Battle of Fort Blakeley, the 114th briefly moved to Selma and Montgomery. It ended its duty in July in Galveston, Texas.[57]

Major Ephraim Brown

"About 5 o'clock…Col. Moore…told me to notify the pickets that they were to fall in on the left side of the 83rd Ohio Regiment…all things were soon made ready and we were both skirmishers and column were in the rifle pit nearest the enemies works which was about 700 yards distant. Between us and the rebel works was a lot of fallen timber and three abatis.…We sat in the ditch a few minutes awaiting the signal to start. It was given and the skirmishers bounded forward. The rebs opened a volley of musketry on us.…The skirmishers ran forward. My men having the best ground got a considerable distance before the 83rd on our right were crossing a bushy hollow and for a short time we received a cross fire from the rebs though we crouched down by the logs and stumps until our right end of the line came up. We then arose and all ran to the rebel forts and breastworks. The rebs kept up their fire until our men were to their works when the whole column sprang from the rifle pit with a yell. They rushed forward and so frightened the rebs that they surrendered to the skirmishers.…Several of the skirmishers that started through with me fell to rise no more."[58]

83RD OHIO VOLUNTEER INFANTRY

The 83rd Ohio was organized in the late summer of 1862 near Cincinnati and originally attached to the Army of Kentucky. It participated in the Yazoo Expedition in the winter of 1862–63, seeing action at Milliken's Bend and Chickasaw Bayou and participating in the assault on Fort Hindman in Arkansas in January 1863. The unit was involved in the entirety of the actions of the Vicksburg campaign, from April to July 1863, and was part of the forces that laid siege to Jackson, Mississippi, afterward. Sent to Louisiana at the completion of those operations, the 83rd took park in the Red River campaign in 1864. It advanced on Fort Blakeley from Pensacola as part of General Steele's column in the spring of 1865. The 83rd was mustered out of service at Galveston in July 1865.[59]

Private C.W. Gerard

"[G]rape and canister had done their work, and many brave boys lay dead and wounded. Up jumped the fortunate ones in another instant; and now, see! They are up the works, and look! There go the reserves after them on the run! Their officers cannot keep them back, and they run on, deaf, as it were, to order and ordnance. Hark! Do you hear that cheer? It is scarcely twenty minutes since our skirmishers advanced, and now they are inside the works and their supporting column are climbing the parapet in swarms! Who ever saw a sight that surpassed that in point of bravery, alacrity and determination?"[60]

Private Isaac Jackson

"About 5 p.m. we are ordered into the front rifle pits. We knew what was coming next, of course. It would be a charge on the rebel works.…At

Regimental flag of the 83rd Ohio Infantry. *State of Ohio Adjutant General's Battle Flag Collection.*

about 15 min. before 6 p.m. we were to start. I never saw the boys in better spirits nor seem cooler than they did when they were looking for the word 'forward.' Everything was done with the greatest of quietness. The rebel works were about 600 or 700 yds. from us with fallen timber all the way across and other obstructions that we knew nothing of. Presently the word came, and over we went with a whoop running as fast as possible. There was but little firing by the skirmish line but the Rebs piled it in thick and fast. We ran about 1/3 of the way and stopped for breath and then up again and for the fort. This 'heat' we crossed a ravine and took breath on top of the hill. Then up and for another run. We had just come through an abatis of brush. On the top of this hill was another (but more dense than the first) and a short distance from that was the third one—more formidable than the other two, being composed of short stubby pine limbs and long sharpened stakes in with it. Between the 2nd and 3rd was a wire stretched so as to throw a man on those sharp stakes. But it was a little too far off for the purpose intended. The wire tripped nearly every man. I did not see it. I must have jumped in running."[61]

34TH IOWA INFANTRY

The 34th Iowa entered service in October 1862 and was first stationed in Helena, Arkansas. It saw action in the Yazoo Expedition, the Battle of Chickasaw Bayou and the capture of Fort Hindman prior to being sent to guard captured Confederates at Union prisons. It returned to the Mississippi Valley in 1863 and participated in the Vicksburg campaign, after which it saw service in Louisiana and Texas. It took part in operations against Fort Gaines and Fort Morgan in August 1864. After the Battle of Fort Blakeley, the 34th mustered out of service in August 1865.[62]

Captain J.S. Clark

"[F]ive p.m of the 9th was fixed as the time for general assault on the enemy's works. At that hour the simultaneous firing of all the cannon on the line was to be the signal for the charge. Our troops had all been formed in line of battle in the entrenchments nearest the enemy, with bayonets fixed.…Breathlessly all awaited the signal to move forward. The silence was interrupted only by an occasional shot from a Confederate picket. The waiting and suspense was a severe test of courage. Some tried to conceal their anxiety by an effort to appear reckless, careless, and brave; they whispered jokes and witticisms pretending that they enjoyed it immensely. Others, more candid and serious, gave their comrades messages to be delivered to loved ones at home in case they fell…

With the crash of signal guns, our first line of skirmishers leaped from the trenches and with yells rushed forward 150 yards, where the second line soon joined them, when all rushed forward together. Now, every cannon the enemy had on his line, and every rifle, poured forth their deadly missiles on our advancing men. Tempests of bullets, pieces of bursting shell, grape and canister filled the air and whistled about our ears. We were met by deadly, unseen and unknown dangers in sunken torpedoes, which, when trodden upon, exploded stripping the flesh from the legs and wounding terribly those not killed outright. Fallen trees, abatis and wire stretched along near the ground, impeded our progress and exposed us longer to the enemy's destructive fire. No reply was made to their guns except by our

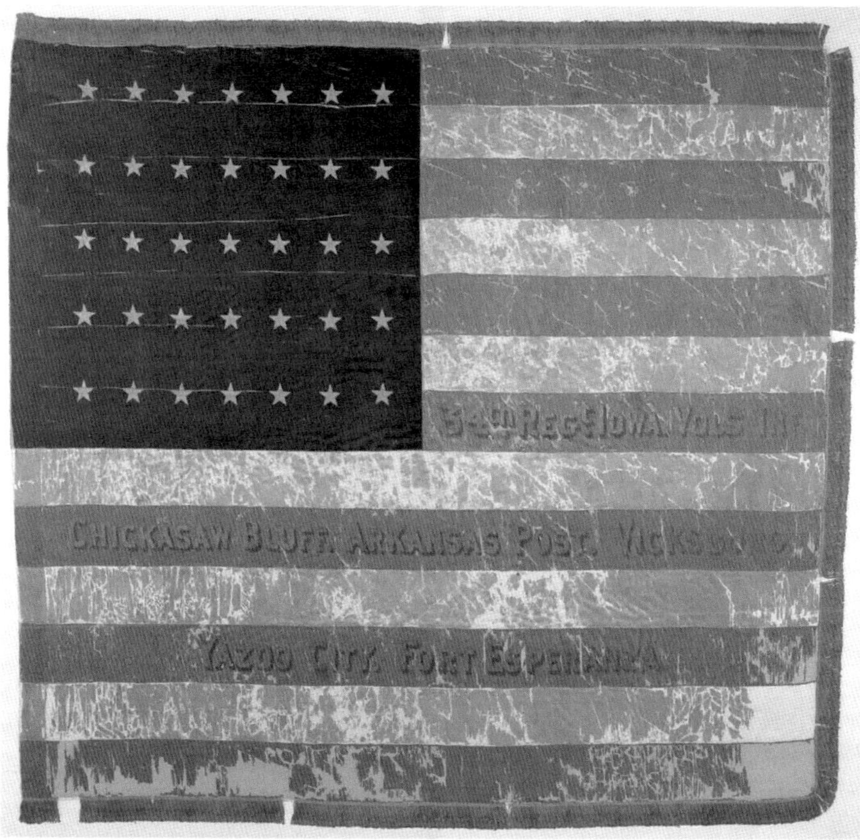

National flag carried by the 34th Iowa. *State Historical Museum of Iowa, Des Moines.*

artillery, which pounded away over our heads with great effect. In twenty minutes we had surmounted all obstacles, climbed over the enemy's works and given him the bayonet."[63]

2nd Division, XIII Corps
Spicely's Brigade

Colonel William T. Spicely

"On the 9th instant, at 5:30 p.m., I received orders from Brig. Gen. C.C. Andrews, commanding Second Division, to place my command in the front parallel of intrenchments, and to deploy one regiment as skirmishers, and to immediately advance upon the works of the enemy. It required but a few moments to form the line. These arrangements for the assault were hardly complete when the gallant Vifquain with his brave boys of the 97th with cheers dashed forward, driving the enemy's line of skirmishers inside of their works. His command was closely followed by the rest of my command, and the contest for a time seemed to be who should arrive in the enemy's works first. The dash was so sudden and impetuous that it was almost impossible to determine who arrived first. But the honor of first entering the works is justly due to the 97th Illinois on the left, and to the 76th Illinois, led by the gallant Busey, on the right, the 24th and 69th Indiana at or about the same time.... The contest was short and decisive; the enemy threw down their arms and surrendered, my command capturing several hundred prisoners, among the number General Cockrell."[64]

97TH ILLINOIS INFANTRY

The 97th Illinois was organized at Camp Butler, Illinois, in 1862. Early in the war, it served in Kentucky and Tennessee prior to participating in the Yazoo Expedition and the Vicksburg campaign. Following Vicksburg's capture, the regiment helped lay siege to Jackson. Following action in the Red River campaign, it was sent to Pascagoula, from which it moved to Pensacola to join Steele in time for his advance on Blakeley. The 97th went to Selma and Cahawba after Blakeley's capture and ended the war in Galveston, Texas.[65]

Sergeant Carlos W. Colby

"[F]ort Blakeley…had all manner of obstructions known…for killing, maiming and obstructing progress. Scores of torpedoes were planted in the ground, fallen timber, and abatis, were part of the defense we had to charge over. On April 9 the charge was made. In just 11 minutes, the left wing of our forces entered the works. The 97th flag being one of the first planted on the fort, but the color-bearer fell mortally wounded. His last words were 'Col., I raised the flag on the works, it is all that I can do.' When near the fort, and I on top of a line of abatis, several feet from the ground, a cannon to our right threw in a murderous volley of canister, two of the shot passing through my clothes, and the third striking the lock of my gun, firing it off and breaking the stock. Seeing a man fall at my left, I started to get his gun, but while in the act, I received a gun shot wound through the muscles of the right leg, partially severing three of the ligaments. Crawling back to a place of safety, I had the grand and thrilling sight of a charge of a colored brigade off to the right; saw dropping forward out of sight as a volley of canister passed over them, then up and onward with thinned ranks, always keeping an eye on the guns for smoke—again to fall as the charge passed over them. As the storming column passed over the works, I could distinctly hear their yell 'Fort Pillow, Fort Pillow.'"[66]

Lieutenant Colonel Victor Vifquain

"On the 9th of April, at 5 pm, I received instructions to deploy my regiment as skirmishers in front of our brigade and to charge the enemy at 5:30 pm. At 5:30 pm precisely my regiment assaulted the enemy, and five minutes afterward my flag waved on the rebel works; the enemy making a most terrible resistance, and our advance impeded by artificial obstructions, my loss was rather heavy, going into battle with about 500 men and losing 61 killed and wounded....My regiment captured 1 battle-flag, 1 headquarters flag (French's division), and another battle-flag (Missouri brigade, General Cockrell's).[67]

Private James M. Dunn

"At about 6 o'clock the charge began and within twenty minutes all was ours....Our loss has been light compared with the value of the results. We believe we now have the key to Mobile and the Confederacy is certainly on its expiring couch. Long may it expire! The 97th led the charge and gained the parapet in less than 13 minutes. It lost five commanding officers wounded... nine men killed....Noble dead! Heroic wounded! Your names shall not be unremembered."[68]

First Sergeant W.R. Eddington

"Well the time has come for the great charge to be made and well we know that many of us will never see the light of another day for our eyelids will be closed in death. We have come to the hours that try men's souls and although it is now more than 69 years ago since this happened, as I go back and call to memory those scenes over again the tears are running down over my cheeks so fast they blind my eyes and I have to stop and wipe them away...

About 5 o'clock, April 9, 1865, the drums sounded the long roll which is the signal for everyone to fall in line. We have just got our coffee for supper. We sat down in our tents, grabbed our guns and fell in line and they rushed us up to the front and into the rifle pits. In a few minutes we got orders to charge. As we got out of the rifle pits the captain of Co. D. struck a torpedo and it blew his leg off below the knee and sent it up in the air about 50 feet high, and my captain who stood next to me on my right was shot through the left shoulder. I and two of my boys made for the skirmish pit. There was a Rebel major and two privates in it. The privates jumped out and ran back toward the Rebel line but the major stayed and kept on shooting. We jumped down on top of him. We picked him up and threw him out of the hole and told him to go to the rear. He started to go but turned as if to come back but our Colonel caught him by the coat collar and forced him to the rear. Just then another of my boys came along and just as he got to the bank of the pit they shot him through the body just at the belt line and he fell down in the pit right on top of me....I had not gone far when a man next to me on my left stepped on a torpedo with his left foot. It blew his left leg off below the knee, his right leg off above the knee and passed up between his head and mine and never touched me...

We went on and when we was within about 20 yards of their works they poured a volley into us which riddled our flag, cut the staff off about two feet from the top. We went on through that withering fire which greeted us from the Rebel guns. We went over the ditch, over their breastworks and jumped down in the rifle pits on top of them too close to shoot them, too close to stick them with our bayonets, but we could still use the butts of our guns. We ordered them to throw their guns outside the breastworks which they did and then we gathered them up in groups and put guards around them until we could get things straightened out. Our color bearer was killed on the breastworks. He had taken the flag staff out of the leather socket in the belt that goes around the waist and was holding it in his hands. He was shot right through the body while standing on the Rebel breastworks."[69]

69TH INDIANA INFANTRY

The 69th Indiana Infantry was organized at Richmond, Indiana, in August 1862 and originally attached to the Army of Kentucky. It took part in the Battle of Richmond, Kentucky, August 29–30, 1862, where it was captured. After being paroled, it was reorganized at Indianapolis and sent to take part in Sherman's Yazoo Expedition in the winter of 1862–63. The regiment took part in the capture of Fort Hindman in January 1863 and went on to serve throughout the Vicksburg campaign. It served in a variety of posts in Louisiana and Texas afterward, seeing action in the Red River campaign. The 69th was sent to Dauphin Island in December 1864 and participated in Granger's Pascagoula Expedition that month before being sent to Pensacola. After the fall of Fort Blakeley, it marched to Selma and Montgomery but returned to Mobile Bay in May. It mustered out of service in July 1865.[70]

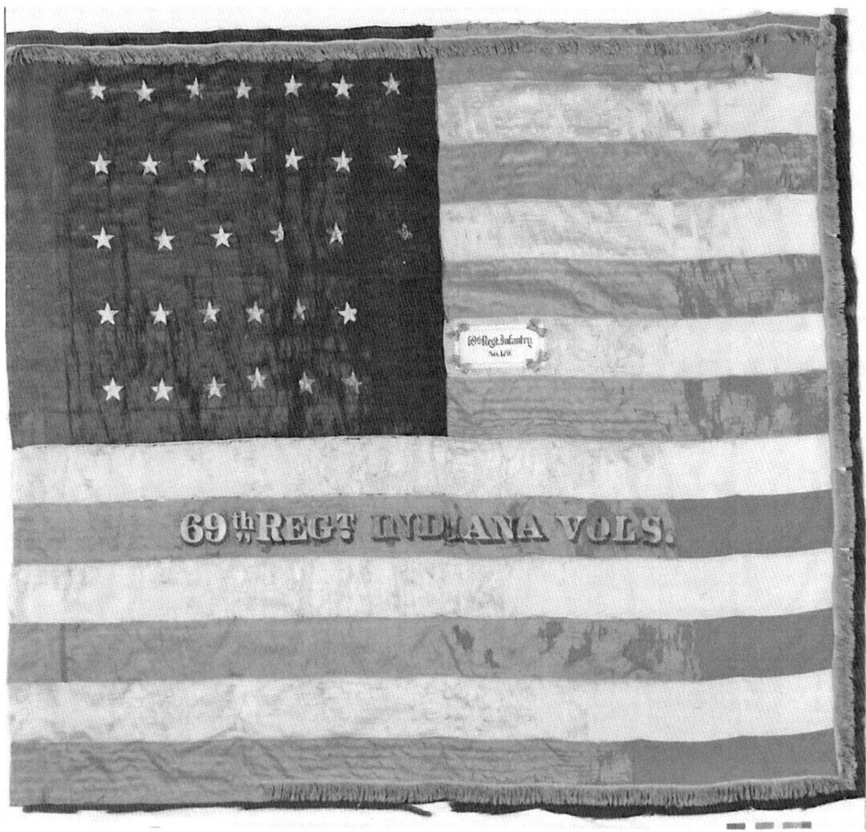

National flag carried by the 69th Indiana Infantry. *Indiana War Memorial.*

Private S.G. Schlagle

"Saturday the 16th Corps arrived and on Sunday even[ing] at 5½ o'clock on the 9th of April the [w]hole line was ordered to mak[e] a grand asalt on the enemy's work and at half past five the 97th Ill up front with the 24th and then the 76th and then the 69th with our brave colonel with his glittering sword unsheathed waved it in the air and call out 69th fall in men. They sprang from the rifle pits and not waiting for nothing in double quick and then in a run for the Works. On yet and still on until they was up to the very jaws of death into the very gates of hell gone through. Smoke and fire grape and canister musket ball flew thick and fast. Hark the brave boys ar[e] charging and have comenst [*sic*] climbing the Works. It is scarce 20 minutes since the skirmishers started and now they ar[e] inside of the works. Whoever saw sich [*sic*] a sight that surpassed that in point of bravery and with alacrity and determination. And what is the result of that breaf [*sic*] half hours work? The compleat [*sic*] possession of the line of earth works bastions and the fort."[71]

Captain John Macey
"This 9th day of April (1865) was on Sunday, and as a custom of some of the boys were writing home, some were washing their clothes, others were discussing the results of the heavy cannonading at Spanish Fort the evening before....At half past five the signal guns were fired, and no sooner fired than the Colonel of the 97th Illinois, who had been designated to take the advance and deploy his regiment with the advance of our division, drew his sword and gave the command, 'Forward!' Every man leapt from the trenches to the exposed ground in front of our lines; deployed as skirmishers they picked their way as best they could through brush. Return fire was immediate. Shells burst, minnie-balls whizzed by; leaden curtains were blazing death hails...shredding flesh, sewing carnage!... We had not gone twenty yards until many had fallen. The fusillade was unremitting...ripping bodies athwart as rag dolls!...Neither can language justly describe so piteous and ever-changing a scene as this!... Smoke, slaughter, screaming men! Blood, sweat, quick death and slow!— No words in Man's language are exact enough! Or too cruel enough in precision! Bloodbath is mere elocution, formed in letters! Hideous is not too harsh—and falls short also!"[72]

76TH ILLINOIS VOLUNTEER INFANTRY
Organized at Kankakee, Illinois, the 76th was stationed at various points in Tennessee prior to service in the Vicksburg campaign and the siege of Jackson. Afterward, it saw action in Louisiana, capturing Fort Beauregard and then moving back into Mississippi during the Meridian campaign of early 1864. The regiment was sent to New Orleans in late 1864, and in January 1865, it moved to Mobile Point before joining Steele's men at Pensacola. Following the capture of Fort Blakeley and the fall of Mobile, the 76th briefly occupied the city before being sent to Selma. It mustered out of service at Galveston in July 1865.[73]

Colonel S.T. Busey
"On the afternoon of the 9th instant orders were received that an advance would be made at 5 o'clock. I took my position in the third parallel on the right center of the brigade, and when ordered advanced, passing the

A monument to the service of the 76th Illinois stands amid the graves of its troops who died during the Mobile campaign at the Mobile National Cemetery. *Historic Blakeley State Park.*

Regimental flag of the 76th Illinois Infantry. *Illinois State Military Museum, Springfield.*

skirmishers at the first abatis, arriving at the enemy's works in advance of any other troops, where we planted our colors (which were almost severed from the staff) fifty yards left of the bastion on our right. After planting our colors on the parapet one of the color guard took them, went to the bastion on our right, walking on the parapet, and while planting them there was knocked senseless by the concussion of a gun fired, falling inside with the colors in his arms, where he was killed by a rebel officer....I claim for my command the honor of first entering the enemy's works and planting our colors thereon."[74]

24TH INDIANA INFANTRY

The 24th Indiana organized at Vincennes in July 1861. It served under General John C. Frémont in Missouri during the first year of the war, afterward moving to Tennessee, where it joined Grant's army in time for action at the Battle of Shiloh. It then participated in the Siege of Corinth prior to moving into Arkansas early in 1863. The 24th took part in the Vicksburg campaign and then served at several stations in Louisiana throughout 1864. It was transferred to Pensacola in January 1865. It was sent to Selma after the fall of Blakeley and mustered out of service in November 1865 at Galveston.[75]

Lieutenant Colonel Francis A. Sears

"When the assault was determined upon every officer and man was at his post, and when the signal for the advance was given they moved with the calm courage and determination of veteran soldiers. In consequence of the nature of the ground over which we passed a perfect line was not maintained. The enemy had placed every obstacle in the way of our advance. Trees felled with branches outward, and torpedoes planted in the supposed path an assaulting column would take, and the sharp fire of musketry, shell, and canister, which the enemy kept up, were not sufficient to deter the regiment from its impetuous advance."[76]

Private Richard J. Fulfer

"Our skirmish line was ordered to charge all along our lines at 5 o'clock. We had to go two hundred fifty yards, through three picket fences and over hundreds of torpedoes, to gain their main forts. I was on the skirmish line, and looking back, I saw our entire force coming, everyone trying to get across that field of death and destruction. At first many brave comrades planted their colors on the rebel fortifications, to pitch over into the rifle pits, with a bullet crashing through their heads. Scores were blown out of existence by torpedoes, the air was full of canister and minnie balls, but the work was short and decisive....This charge lasted about fifty minutes. The rebel troops in front of the colored troops surrendered to our division, for they knew that the negroes would not show them any quarters, as they came up with the shout of 'Fort Pillow,' and they continued to shoot at the rebels even after they raised the white flags."[77]

2ND CONNECTICUT LIGHT ARTILLERY

The 2nd Connecticut Light Artillery Battery was organized at Bridgeport in August 1862. It served in Virginia and around Washington, D.C., in 1863 as a reserve unit of the Army of the Potomac. The battery saw heavy action in the Battle of Gettysburg in July 1863, going from there to New York to help keep order during rioting associated with implementation of the draft before returning to Washington. It was sent to New Orleans in 1864 and stationed at various posts in Louisiana prior to being sent to Mobile Bay to assist in capturing Fort Morgan and Fort Gaines. It advanced on Blakeley from Pensacola and, after the battle there, continued in service until being mustered out in August 1865.[78]

Private William J. Gould
"A staff officer came around and gave us orders to fire regular all day as the Johnyes [*sic*] were evacuating….We kept firing at them all day making some splendid shots but receiving no reply. At 5 o'clock our boys were to charge the works and none of the battery boys having seen one we all waited with anxious expectations to see it. A few minutes before a staff officer came around and ordered us to cease firing. At 5 o'clock our boys started. They had between 300 and 400 hundred yards to run. They had to stop and rest once. It was the greatest site I ever saw….I jumped and cheered with all my might. Success crowned our efforts. Their whole line of works was carried….Many of our boys were blown up with torpedoes."[79]

Corporal W.H. Hart
"After firing all day yesterday, the order came at 5 o'clock to cease firing. We began to wonder what was up. Soon we heard a yell and increased firing by the rebs. We looked over the works and our entire line from right to left was charging the reb works. We had a good view. It was a glorious sight, a line of 15,000 men marching steady into the jaws of death. At one time the line wavered in our front but they rallied and soon the Star Spangled Banner in triumph did wave over the rebel works. When that line was moving up, I lived years. I had no control of myself. Though the reb bullets was flying thick and fast over us, yet we mounted our works and yelled like fiends almost….They have in the vicinity of their works filled in with torpedoes….I think it is not civilized….I counted 15 in a space about 50 feet in diameter. While counting, I found myself standing astride one, my right foot being about 3 inches from the cap….A captain had his leg blown off the first step he took after leaving the rifle pits to charge. Another had both legs blown off besides his private parts was all blown off….Our men suffered more by these devilish things than by rifle fire. They was exploding all the time during the charge….General Steele is making the prisoners take them up. Two of them have been killed. Amen."[80]

Confederate Lines

1ST MISSOURI BRIGADE

The 1st Missouri Brigade was formed in early 1862 from several existing veteran units, including the 1st Missouri Cavalry, 2nd Missouri Infantry and 3rd Missouri Infantry. Over the course of the ensuing years of the war, it forged a reputation for itself as perhaps the most dependable and hardest-fighting unit in the western Confederacy. The brigade's list of actions is a veritable enumeration of Western Theater battles; it fought with distinction at the Battles of Pea Ridge, Shiloh, Iuka, Corinth, the several battles of the Vicksburg campaign, the several actions of the Atlanta campaign and the Battles of Franklin and Nashville. Following its capture at Vicksburg in July 1863, the brigade was paroled and reorganized. Due to attrition, several of its units were at that time consolidated. Portions of the command present at Blakeley include the 1st and 3rd Missouri Cavalry (dismounted), the 1st and 4th Missouri Infantry, the 2nd and 6th Missouri Infantry and the 3rd and 5th Missouri Infantry.[81]

2ND AND 6TH CONSOLIDATED REGIMENT, MISSOURI INFANTRY

This consolidated regiment was composed of elements of the 2nd and 6th Missouri Infantry regiments, which had been reorganized in October 1863. The 2nd Missouri had been formed at Springfield in January 1862 and fought at Pea Ridge, Iuka, Corinth and Vicksburg prior to the reorganization. The 6th Missouri was organized in May 1862 and had a similar history of engagements. As a consolidated unit, the regiment fought in the Atlanta and Nashville campaigns before being sent to the Mobile area in early 1865.[82]

Corporal William H. Kavanaugh

"On the 8th day of April it fell my lot to go on the skirmish line, for the first time since my return....Our instructions were that in case the enemy advanced on us in heavy bodies to stand our ground and fight them back as long as possible, then if need be, surrender to them. I made up my mind then and there not to surrender to any one or to any body of men as long as there was the ghost of a chance to escape. Just the thought of going back to prison made me desperate....Tomorrow came. It was the 9th day of April, 1865....But we knew nothing of Lee's surrender doings at this time....From my view point, could be seen his [Canby's] right wing circle around our left and double it back on the center. This being accomplished, they then

Flag of the 2nd and 6th Consolidated Infantry. *Missouri State Museum, Missouri State Parks.*

advanced in our immediate front in solid columns. An imposing sight, truly, was this, and one never to be forgotten. Our little thin line of skirmishers loaded and fired as rapidly as possible, but on they came as though no one could harm them. After firing eight or ten rounds in rapid succession, and the advance line within 150 yards of our position and seeing the utter uselessness of our efforts to check them, I hurriedly told my companions that for one I was going to make a break and try to save myself—they could do as they pleased....When we emerged from the pit we were in full view of the enemy, and, as we were making as fast time as our feeble bodies would allow, it appeared to me that all hell had turned loose and that every man in the United States was practicing on us with repeating rifles."[83]

1st and 3rd Consolidated Regiment Missouri Cavalry (Dismounted)

This consolidated regiment was composed of elements of the 1st and 3rd Missouri Cavalry Regiments, which served at Blakeley as infantry. The 1st Missouri Cavalry had been formed in 1861 and fought at Pea Ridge, Iuka and Corinth prior to the reorganization of the brigade in the fall of 1863.

Flag of the 1st Missouri Cavalry, Dismounted. *Missouri State Museum, Missouri State Parks.*

The 3rd Missouri Cavalry, organized in the summer of 1862 after the Battle of Pea Ridge, had a similar service record. As a consolidated unit, the 1st and 3rd took part in the Atlanta and Nashville campaigns prior to being sent to the trenches at Blakeley.[84]

Captain Joseph Boyce
"[T]he men felt able to repulse any force which could be massed in their front. At this moment the men of the First Missouri regiment were amazed to see a line of the enemy at their rear with guns levelled and crying out Surrender! They hesitated only a moment, when Lt. Harry Thompson, of Co. E cried out to Major Charles L. Edmondson, commanding the regiment 'Is it fight or surrender? Talk quick Major' Poor Edmondson, brave hearted always, took a look at the enemy, dropped his sword point to the ground, saying 'surrender.' The fight was over, and with it I may say the war."[85]

Corporal Ephraim McDonald Anderson
"On the ninth of April Blakeley was attacked by a strong Federal force. The position of our brigade was in the line of earthworks near the center, with troops from other commands upon each side of it.…The Federal command

Captain Joseph Boyce, Company D, 1st Missouri. *Missouri History Museum.*

in front of our brigade was repulsed and driven back with heavy loss; the attack was renewed, but the position was firmly held. Shoulder to shoulder, with courage that never yielded, the repeated assaults were withstood.... In this critical juncture a Federal brigade, which had succeeded in getting into the works, made a rapid movement and came up in the rear, while our brigade was still fighting in front, and drawing its guns down upon it at the distance of ten paces, called on the command to surrender. Down in the works as it was, and hemmed in on all sides by Federal bayonets, there was no alternative left but to yield to inevitable circumstances. The colors were lowered and the command was surrendered prisoners of war."[86]

First Lieutenant Charles Boarman Cleveland

"At Blakeley we were outnumbered and compelled to surrender....After we had surrendered, the Yankees ran up in our front and began firing on us, killing Captain Niel [Neal] and four of our men. I had been placed in command of Company C, the color company, and, that our chances for life were small, ordered the men to grab their guns and go at them. This we did, killing all that who had come over. Our flag was still ours and I took it from the staff and gave it to one of the men, who afterwards gave it to Colonel Gates."[87]

Chapter 3

The Battle of Fort Blakeley

The Fight at Redoubts 1 and 2

Redoubts 1 and 2, the northernmost reach of the lines at Fort Blakeley, are located north of the park in a private residential area in the vicinity of Newberry Bluff Circle and Newberry Road. The park owns a portion of Redoubt 2, but much of Redoubt 1 has been lost to development. (Visitors interested in seeing the section of Redoubt 2 owned by the park are asked to inquire with park staff before exploring the area on their own.) Perched on the brow of a bluff overlooking the Tensaw and relatively closer together than other sections of the Confederate line, in the immediate front of these redoubts was a short, sloping plain that rose gradually in the distance to higher ground on which Confederates had cleared timber for several yards. These two positions were under continuous assault for a longer period of time than any other section of the fort during the battle on April 9, 1865.

Attacking along this section of the line were nine regiments of United States Colored Troops (USCT) under the overall divisional command of Brigadier General John P. Hawkins. Comprising for the most part former slaves primarily hailing from Louisiana and Missouri, the majority of these units had been in service less than two years. While a few had seen major fighting, most had taken part in only occasional skirmishing during duty at various points on the Mississippi from Vicksburg to Port Hudson. Facing them would be remnants of several veteran Confederate units cobbled together into the lines at Blakeley, primarily Alabama and Mississippi men who had witnessed some of the major actions of the Western Theater. There

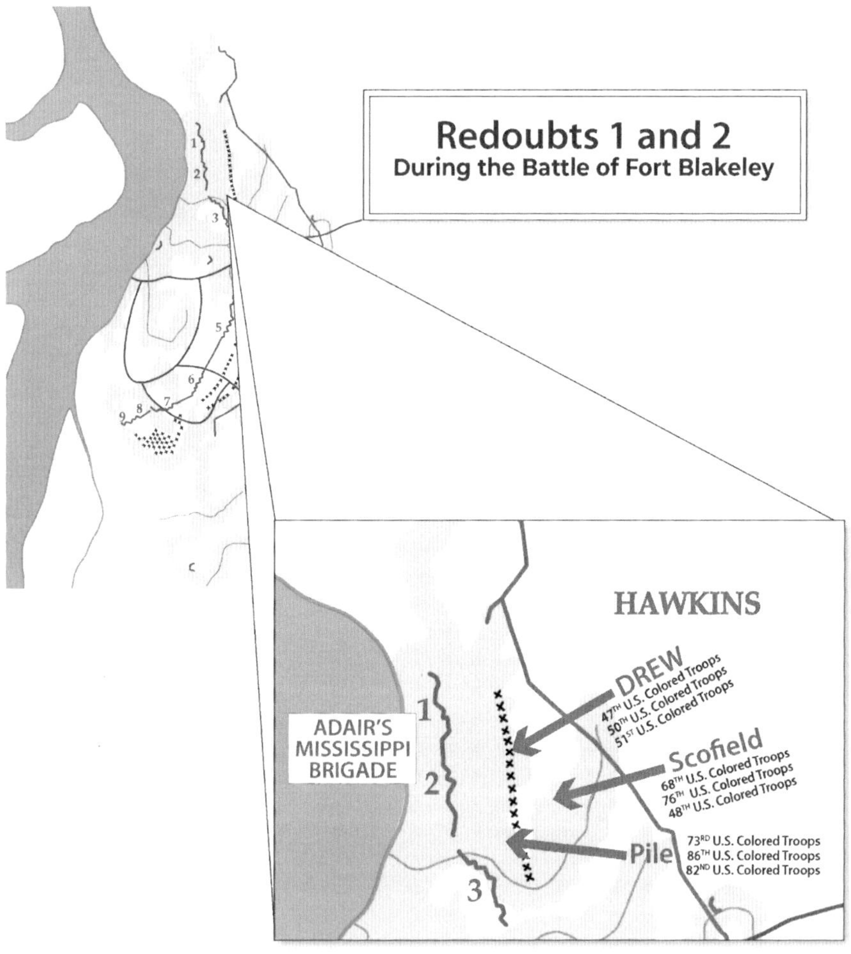

Redoubts 1 and 2 during the Battle of Fort Blakeley. *Historic Blakeley State Park.*

was a great disparity in numbers; nearly five thousand USCT troops would be attacking perhaps five hundred Confederates.[88]

After learning of the evacuation of Spanish Fort on the night of April 8, the Union command at Blakeley became apprehensive that the Rebels they were besieging might likewise attempt to give them the slip and thus render meaningless more than a week of hard fighting. They carefully observed activity in the fort during the day, watching anxiously for any sign of evacuation. When the skirmishers in the advanced rifle pits in front of Redoubts 1 and 2 suddenly fell silent a little after noon on April 9, some officers in the ranks of the USCT regiments wondered what the break in the action might mean. A small group of officers, led by Lieutenant Colonel Merriam of the 73rd USCT, by early afternoon had obtained permission to take a small force on a daring reconnaissance mission closer to the fort to determine what was going on. At about 3:00 p.m., a select group of men from the 86th and 73rd USCT probed the Confederate line in front of Redoubts 1 and 2, exposing themselves in daring fashion and taking many casualties as they ran through areas of felled timber and up to the crest of the rise on which sat some of the outermost rifle pits.[89]

The Confederates, believing the bold reconnaissance to be the prelude to a major attack, rushed what reinforcements they could muster in this sector to Redoubts 1 and 2. The Federal command responded in kind, and soon a raging firefight was underway. After a prolonged period of disorganized firing from short range, the Rebel skirmishers fell back into their main line. At about 4:00 p.m., Colonel Charles W. Drew ordered his men to advance up to the Confederate works. His command at once "broke off on the double-quick with shouts, and charged with the greatest enthusiasm." The fort's defenders responded with a ferocious fire that cut down many of the attackers and stalled the advance. Drew then ordered his men to the right, so as to approach Redoubt 1 from the edge of the bluff on which it sat, as a small ravine and thick brush would provide it more cover.[90]

The Federals got within fifty yards of the redoubt, where a small depression allowed a measure of protection while "a storm of missiles was still sweeping over them." But once there, they found themselves in a dangerous dilemma. Numbering fewer than one hundred men in all, they had insufficient force to mount a direct charge on the fortification and would surely suffer horrific casualties should they attempt to retreat back across the open ground. The Confederates, at that time taking fire from their front and their flank, attempted a sally to disperse the obstinate attackers and at one point placed a small howitzer in front of the redoubt to sweep the brush where the Federals fired intermittently from concealment. They were forced to abandon both efforts and return to the safety of the main line in short order, but the stalemate continued. With no reserve available to press the advance in front of the redoubts, Lieutenant Colonel Daniel Densmore of the 68th USCT ordered his men to fall back in an orderly fashion at about 5:00 p.m., collecting their dead and wounded as they went. Confederate gunboats in the Tensaw attempted to shell them once they were far enough away from the main line to not endanger the defenders of the fort with their fire, but most of the shells missed the mark. During the whole affair, the advanced elements of the reconnaissance party remained in place on the bluff mere yards from the flank of Redoubt 1.[91]

A desultory firefight continued for another half hour until the roars of the wave of cheering Federals to the left of the USCT's position could be heard at about 5:45 p.m. Seeing the men of the 2nd Division making their assault on Redoubts 3 and 4 in the distance, Brigadier General William A. Pile at once ordered his men forward. Within moments, all of Hawkins's division was in motion in a spirited charge, with the lead elements covering for a second time a portion of the field between the lines of the opposing armies. "Greater gallantry than was shown by officers and men could hardly be desired," remembered one federal officer. "The latter were burning with an impulse to do honor to their race, and rushed forward with intense enthusiasm, in face of a terrible fire." The 73rd USCT was credited with being the first unit to place its colors on the Confederate works in this sector, on Redoubt 2.[92]

Owing to the unique dynamic of the contest at Redoubts 1 and 2, which was waged by white Confederates against black troops led by white officers, the fight on this part of the line was characterized by a particular bitterness and desperation. Many of the fort's defenders were incredulous that black troops were being sent against them. In the last moments of the fight, as their position was being overrun, some of the Confederates in this sector ran toward Redoubt 3 to surrender to white troops, as they either feared that their rights as prisoners would not be respected or wanted to avoid the perceived indignity of being captured by black soldiers. The USCT troops who participated in the early afternoon reconnaissance could hear some of the racial epithets being uttered within the fort about their presence on the battlefield—according to Brigadier General Andrews, men of the 51st USCT could hear a Confederate officer ordering his men to "lay low and mow the ground—the damned niggers are coming"—but none of the USCT troops present needed any insults to stoke the racial tension heavy in the air. Most were former slaves with little heavy combat experience and fervently desired to prove themselves in battle against men they believed desired to keep them in bondage. The intrepidity of their assault proved their courage without any doubt.[93]

Accounts of events that took place in the closing moments of the battle, though, have unfortunately cast their efforts with an unsavory tinge of disorderliness virtually since the last shots were fired. Legend, based to some degree on exaggerated claims published decades later, has long held that surrendering Confederates were wantonly gunned down in Redoubts

Sketch of the area in front of Redoubts 1 and 2 as it appeared in 1866. *From* The Campaign of Mobile.

1 and 2 by USCT troops. Available evidence, some of which is included in the following accounts of Union officers and Confederate troops, does show that a few renegade individuals from USCT ranks attempted to shoot down some soldiers in the act of surrendering. Two USCT officers were wounded, one mortally, in attempting to restrain their men in the chaotic last moments of the fight as defeated Confederates laid down their arms. Order was quickly restored, however, and there was no coordinated or sanctioned massacre, as some have later alleged. One soldier from the 50th USCT, in fact, is reputed to have spotted his former master among the captives, and the two shared a drink of water from his canteen. Their wonder at the extraordinary turn of events in Southern society that had just played out in one of the war's last battles, while beyond the scope of this guide, can only be imagined.[94]

IN THEIR OWN WORDS

UNITED STATES COLORED TROOPS (USCT)

The United States Colored Troops (USCT) comprised regiments of the U.S. Army with African American soldiers. While the majority of the men in the ranks were former slaves, white officers commanded all units in combat. The Federal government had first authorized acceptance of small numbers of Black regiments in specific locations in the fall of 1862, but after the Emancipation Proclamation went into effect on January 1, 1863, it began actively recruiting African American soldiers. Organization of these units was overseen by the Bureau of Colored Troops, formed later in 1863, which arranged for the enlistment, outfitting and training of numerous new Black regiments. By April 1865, there were more than 180,000 USCT troops in the Federal army, which represented about 10 percent of its total manpower. USCT regiments participated in most of the major campaigns of the final two years of the Civil War and frequently took part in combat, although in many cases they were used only for supply and guard details or manual labor. Their presence at Blakeley marks one of the largest concentrations of Black troops to take part in any battle of the war. Nearly 5,000 USCT troops marched with General Frederick Steele's column as its 1st Division, under the command of Brigadier General John P. Hawkins. These men were organized into three brigades led by General William A. Pile, Colonel Hiram Scofield and Colonel Charles W. Drew.[95]

Brigadier General John P. Hawkins
"On the afternoon of the 9th instant orders were sent to the brigade commanders to strengthen and advance their skirmish lines at 5:30 and drive the enemy as far as possible. Before this order reached them their lines had been put in motion at 5 o'clock, and skirmishing continued until 5:30, when, taking up the yell and forward movement commenced by the other divisions on the left, the whole front, re-enforced with other troops from the rear, went at the works of the enemy and were soon piling over the parapet, and the rebels, confronting us threw down their arms. The prisoners captured amounted to 21 officers and 200 men—a small number, owing to the fact that when entered many of the enemy, fearing the conduct of my troops, ran over to where the white troops were entering."[96]

Pile's Brigade

73rd USCT

The 73rd USCT traces its origins to the 1st Louisiana Native Guards, a Black infantry unit organized for service in New Orleans in 1862. The Guards evolved into the Corps de Afrique, or 1st Regiment of Infantry, one of the

Left: General William A. Pile. *Library of Congress.*

Right: Captain Henry C. Nichols. *From* Deeds of Valor: How America's Heroes Won the Medal of Honor.

first Black regiments in the Union army, in 1863. The 1st Regiment was stationed at Port Hudson before being reorganized as the 73rd USCT in the spring of 1864. It participated in the Red River campaign in the summer of 1864 and then moved to Pensacola. It marched to Blakeley as part of Steele's column in March 1865. After the Battle of Fort Blakeley, the unit moved to Montgomery before returning to Mobile and then was sent for duty in Louisiana, where it remained until September 1865.[97]

Captain Henry C. Nichols

"Between our pits and the abatis was a muddy ravine with a small brook at the bottom, a sharp descent from our pits to the brook, then a plain, gradually ascending to the fort. About 5 o'clock, Colonel Merriam ordered an assault on the outer works by four companies, which was made in fine style, driving the enemy into their main works. The fire from the fort was terrific, and was kept up after the assault, in an attempt to dislodge our men who were lying down on our side of the abatis, quite exposed. It was at this time I volunteered to make a reconnaissance, the colonel wishing to know the nature of the ground he was about to charge over. I ran down into the ravine and reaching the left of the abatis stopped to get my breath.

After resting about a minute I climbed into the branches of a tree and surveyed the field with my glasses. I found the ground favorable for the assault, and returning to my command on a run reported to this effect to the colonel. Colonel Merriam then obtained permission to charge the main works—the fort—and made the assault, followed five or ten minutes later by the rest of the colored division, capturing the works on a run. The ground we traversed and which I had explored had been planted with torpedoes, but this arrangement of the enemy I was not able to detect while on my reconnaissance."[98]

Colonel Henry C. Merriam

Hundred on hundreds fell;
But they are resting well;
Scourges and shackles strong
Shall never do them wrong.
Oh, to the living few,
Soldier, be just and true;
Hail them as comrades tried,
Fight with them side by side,
And never in field or tent
Scorn the Black Regiment

"April 9, we received news of the escape of the garrison of Spanish Fort…during the previous night. The effect upon us all was very depressing, for the failure to capture that garrison after spending half a month digging them out meant that these troops had abandoned a position no longer tenable, only to fall back to stronger fortifications covering Mobile, there to be again besieged, probably under conditions less favorable to us. To me it appeared that the escape of the garrison in our front would be simply disgraceful. Oppressed with this feeling I asked the colonel of the 86th Regiment on my right to go with me to our brigade commander, General Pile, and ask permission to capture the enemy's advanced line of works at once (it was then soon afternoon) instead of waiting for cover of darkness as had been the custom. He [the colonel] refused, and I started alone for headquarters. Before I reached General Pile, however, Major L.P. Mudgett of the 86th, who had heard my interview with his colonel, overtook me and asked to join me in my request. I was, of course, glad to have him do so.…General

Colonel Henry C. Merriam.
Library of Congress.

Pile was quick to appreciate his qualities, and gave him orders to lead his regiment in the voluntary enterprise we had proposed, ignoring his colonel who had refused to join me in the request. Hastening back to the front we made all preparations for the assault as authorized, and so sure was I that my whole regiment would be needed, that I formed it quietly in my advanced parallel, ready for instant call. General Pile's advanced parallel in which we were now formed for attack, was more than one hundred yards nearer the enemy's works than the parallels to our right and left—a circumstance which proved very greatly to our advantage in every stage of the assault which followed…

It was probably about three o'clock when General Pile came to the front to supervise the attack. He was accompanied by Major-General Osterhaus, General Canby's chief of staff. All arrangements being satisfactory, the attack was made with great gallantry by Captain Brown of the 73rd and Captain Jenkins of the 86th. The capture of the outer line was only the work of a few minutes, but so terrific was the fire concentrated upon us from front, and, at first, also from both flanks, by artillery and infantry, and plainly seeing the gathering of reenforcements [*sic*] by the enemy in my front I sent forward as supports Captain Snaer, Company B, Lt. Lyon, Company I, and Company A, Captain Crydenwise, in rapid succession—the last named company taking spades, by order of General Pile, to reverse the captured rifle pits. At this time I hastened to the advance myself. Gallant Major Mudgett had fallen, shot through the head. Captain Brown had fallen mortally wounded and Captain Snaer fell with a severe wound at my feet as I reached the line. He refused to sheathe his sword or to be carried off the field. Captain Crydenwise with his company was reversing the rifle pits. Taking B, G, and I companies under Lt. Lyon—the only officer left in the other brigades of Hawkin's Division were storming the pits in their front and conforming to our lines.

This was about four o'clock, as fixed by the official reports, and these troops had joined in the assault without orders from higher authority, impelled only by that soldierly instinct, which always responds quickly to opportunity. So completely were my skirmishers now in control of the artillery fire in redoubt number two, that I appealed to General Osterhaus for permission to charge the main works with my whole regiment. He refused saying 'I will go and order the white troops up.' I at once appealed to General Pile, emphasizing my request by saying 'We have already fought the battle, but unless we go over the main works we will not get the credit.' He replied, 'You are right, Colonel. When you see Andrews' Division start to advance, charge the main works with your regiment and I will follow you with the rest of the brigade.' I gave the signal and the regiment rushed forward with deafening yells. Our skirmishers joined the ranks as we advanced and all swept over redoubt number two. The enemy were running in disorder to their right, evidently to escape capture by the colored troops, but I was able to cut off a few—two hundred and thirty-four officers and men, all of whom remained under guard of my regiment for that night....Thus ended the assault and capture of Fort Blakeley....It lost much attention and public appreciation through the overshadowing event transpiring in Virginia on the same day—the surrender of Lee—but its place in history, as the last assault of our great and bloody Civil War, will always be assured."[99]

Scofield's Brigade

76th USCT

The 76th USCT was organized in April 1864 as part of the reorganized 4th Corps de Afrique Infantry. It served at Port Hudson until early in 1865, at which time it moved to Pensacola. The regiment advanced on Fort Blakeley from there in March. After the fall of Blakeley, the unit moved to Montgomery and was stationed at various points in central Alabama through the early summer, after which time it was sent to Texas. It ended service on the Rio Grande in December 1865.[100]

Drew's Brigade

Colonel Charles W. Drew

"Sunday, the 9th instant, I ordered the 68th and 76th Regiments (then in the trenches) to double their skirmish lines at 5 pm and drive the enemy from his rifle-pits, and if necessary to do it I should order out the regiments entire. Before the work was fairly commenced, however, I heard cheering on my left and saw the skirmishers of the First Brigade advancing. I immediately gave the command forward, and forward the entire command (except the 48th Reg. left in reserve) swept with a yell. In this advance my extreme right reached a point within 150 feet of the enemy's parapet, but so reduced in numbers and exhausted that I ordered them to fall back to a ravine where they would be safe from the fire of the enemy's gunboats…until I could order up the 48th Regiment and charge the works with some hope of success. Before I could get up with the regiment they had fallen back to the abatis, and when the charge became general they, with the rest, went forward with a shout and did all that brave men could do. The result was soon accomplished and Blakeley was ours."[101]

47th USCT

The 47th USCT traces its origins to the 8th Louisiana Infantry, which was organized at Lake Providence, Louisiana, in the spring of 1863 and saw action in the Vicksburg campaign. In March 1864, it was reorganized as the 47th USCT. The regiment performed garrison duty at Vicksburg until October 1864, when it was sent for operations up the Yazoo River and into Arkansas. In February 1865, the unit was moved to Pensacola and from there advanced on Blakeley. After the battle, the 47th helped occupy Mobile and other points in Alabama before being sent to Texas. It mustered out there in January 1866.[102]

Colonel Hiram Scofield

Colonel Hiram Scofield. *Wikimedia Commons.*

"The ground over which the advances were made was flat and wet and very unfavorable for the health and comfort of the men, confined as they were to the trenches; but stimulated by the love of country and pride of soldiers, neither labor, hunger, nor danger caused any murmurs....Upon this last day of the siege our hearts were made glad by the report of the capture of the Spanish Fort, and each one seemed animated by a desire to emulate the example of our comrades in arms. The enemy's skirmish line yielded less stubbornly today and the artillery fire was not so heavy as formerly. This caused a general belief that the place was being evacuated, and fears were entertained and expressed that the prize was slipping through our fingers. About 4 p.m. the skirmish lines were almost simultaneously advanced around the whole line, and without, so far as I can learn, any orders; and as the enemy rallied, offering a more stubborn resistance, our skirmishers were strengthened, and such was the enthusiasm of the troops that had there been concert of action it is believed the place might then have been captured. As it was the rebels were driven within their works, from which they opened a withering fire of musketry and of grape and canister, temporarily checking the advance. The order was then given to intrench and hold the ground gained. The reserve regiment was then brought up to the advance line of intrenchments. About this time the order came to advance the skirmish line and feel of the enemy's force and position, stating that it was believed the place was being evacuated. This order had been already obeyed, disclosing the fact that the artillery, though before silent, had not been removed, and that there was at least a strong force of the enemy remaining. Just at this time other portions of the line advancing, permission was obtained to move forward and assault the enemy's works. The order was at once given to the 47th and 50th regiments....The command moved with a yell through the abatis and over torpedoes, several of which exploded, driving the rebels from their works and guns, and in conjunction with the regiments of the other brigades which entered the works almost simultaneously, captured a large number of prisoners. The day was won, and Blakeley, with all its garrison and munitions of war, was ours....The spirit and enthusiasm of the troops could not be excelled. Men actually wept that they were placed in reserve and could not go in with their comrades into the thickest of the fight."[103]

51ST USCT

The 51st USCT, the reorganized 1st Mississippi Infantry (African Descent), entered service in March 1864. It was stationed at Vicksburg and along the Mississippi until early 1865, when it moved to Pensacola. The regiment moved from there to Fort Blakeley. After the battle, it occupied Mobile briefly before serving at Montgomery until the summer. It ended its service in Texas in June 1866.[104]

Lieutenant Walter Chapman

"We have been investing this place for 7 days losing more or less men every day until 9th when orders came to advance our skirmishers and support them....As our skirmishers advanced they met a hot reception. Our regiment moved up rapidly to support them. The rebel line of skirmishers seeing us coming up fell back into their works. As soon as our niggers caught sight of the retreating figures of the rebs the very devils could not hold them. Their eyes glittered like serpents and with yells & howls, like hungry wolves, they rushed for the rebel works. The movement was simultaneous. Regt. after regt. and line after line took up the cry and started until the whole field was black with darkeys. The rebs were panic struck. Numbers of them jumped into the river and were drowned in attempting to cross, or were shot while swimming. Still others threw down their arms and run for their lives to the white troops on our left to give themselves up, to save being butchered by our niggers. The niggers did not take a prisoner. They killed all they took to a man. The whole charge was an accident. There were no orders or anything of the kind. They charged without bayonets. I am fully satisfied with them as fighters."[105]

Colonel A. Watson Webber

"On the 9th, at 5 p.m., the regiment was again ordered to the front and participated in the successful assault made upon the enemy's works. While making the charge six men in one company were severely wounded by the explosion of one of the enemy's subterra shells....The gallantry of the officers and men of my command during all the operations was so universal that to enumerate special cases would be invidious. There can be no doubt now, in the minds of their officers at least, but that our colored soldiers are brave and will fight."[106]

Confederate Lines

4TH MISSISSIPPI INFANTRY

The 4th Mississippi was organized at Grenada in 1861 and served in many of the most storied engagements of the Civil War's Western Theater. It participated in the actions at Fort Henry and Fort Donelson in early 1862 and during the numerous actions in the campaign for Vicksburg, where it was captured along with the entirety of the Confederate garrison there. After exchange, it joined the Army of Tennessee and fought in the several battles of the Atlanta campaign and then in the campaign for Nashville. Sent to the defenses of Mobile, the regiment fought in the trenches at Blakeley, where it was captured in its final action.[107]

Private Ben H. Bounds

"There were but 750 of us, but we drove them back three times out of gun shot range. At this junction, the white troops passed over our breastworks to our right and attacked us from the rear when we were

Flag of the 4th Mississippi Infantry. *Mississippi Department of Archives and History.*

forced to surrender. Seeing the white flag the Negro troops came rushing on us with the cry, 'Remember Ft. Pillow.' Had it not been for the white Federal troops and the white officers of the negro regiment, I would not have been here writing this incident. More of our men were slain after the surrender than in the battle. Finally the white officers bunched us in squads of forty or fifty each and placed guards around us as close together as they could stand with fixed bayonets facing outward to protect us from the infuriated mob. They continued to shoot men down, shooting between or over the heads of the guards. Captain Adair fell at my side with a mortal wound. I was caught in the outer edge of my squad when I discovered an infuriated Negro about ten feet from me with his gun on me. I stepped behind the guard. He moved to one side and back again, when I placed the guard between us. At that time a white officer appeared, seeing on his hat the square and compass made with a pencil, I gave him a sign which brought him to my side. I pointed out the Negro and asked him to please not let him kill me as I had fought him like a man, surrendered like a man, would like to be treated like a man. He stepped out and struck the negro on the head with his pistol. The negro turned and ran up on the breastworks. He fired at the negro and I saw him fall over the breastworks. Shortly afterwards the white officer came to my side and asked me if the Negro had bothered me any more. I told him no and was much obliged to him. He whispered to me that he done three others the same way. This shows that Masonry will protect a brother even though he be a foe....In this battle I fired one hundred and ten rounds. Seventy of those rounds were fired when they were within sixty yards of us as thick as blackbirds. I took deliberate aim every time I fired and must have killed $50,000 worth of Negroes that day."[108]

Private Thomas Martin Murphree

"The Confederate line had so few men that they were placed twenty feet distance from each other behind the breastworks....The first charge on the Confederate position was made by regiments of Negro soldiers, the first my father had ever seen in battle....They came yelling and shooting, but they were tangled in the trees, they stepped on the mines, and they were fired upon by the hardy Confederates at such close quarters that they could not miss. The result was a terrible slaughter and the remnants broke and ran away from the battlefield. Then the whole Yankees charged and they too were driven back, but finally using the old tactics with a very largely superior force, the Yankees turned a huge force and came around in behind and on the flank of the Confederate position and hemmed them between these forces so they could neither continue to fight or escape. The Yankee officers called on the Confederates to surrender and they obeyed. Then the command was given to the Confederates to stack their arms—meaning to give up their guns. This order too was obeyed by the Confederates. As soon as they had done this, my father said the Negroes rushed in and began to shoot down the unarmed Confederates in cold blood. He saw several men shot to death in this way. Finally, however, the white Yankee officers began to knock the negroes down with the flats of their swords and finally stopped the massacre."[109]

Tarrant's Battery

Organized at Pollard, Alabama, in June 1863 and under the command of Captain E.W. Tarrant of Tuscaloosa, Tarrant's Battery joined the Army of Tennessee and saw action in the several battles of the Atlanta campaign in the summer of 1864. It went on to fight in the Nashville campaign, where at the Battle of Nashville it lost most of its horses and all of its guns. The unit was transferred to the District of the Gulf afterward, where it was captured at the Battle of Fort Blakeley.[110]

Captain E.W. Tarrant

"[L]ate in the afternoon of Sunday, April 9 [the date of the surrender of Lee at Appomattox] a brigade of Minnesota troops succeeded in breaking through the ranks of Thomas' boy regiment, and, swinging around in the rear of the fort, nothing was left for us except to run up a white flag, a pocket handkerchief so called. Then the negro troops rushed over our works in great rage, accusing us of having fired on them after we had surrendered, shooting down Captain Lanier, inspector general of the Mississippi brigade, and clubbing 'Long' Smith, of Tarrant's Battery. It looked as though we were to be butchered in cold blood, so I passed word along our line that if another man was shot I would seize a musket, as would every man of us, as we would die fighting to the last. The officers of the negroes, however, succeeded in getting control of them, and there were no other outrages. There were two torpedo lines in our front, their location unknown except those who were employed in planting the torpedoes. As the negroes were rushed over these lines, many were killed and wounded by the explosions. A Federal captain told me that in

Captain E.W. Tarrant.
Alabama Department of Archives and History.

their last charge the explosion of one torpedo placed thirteen men of his company *hors de combat*. Many of the Missourians and Mississippians and the boy regiment succeeded in escaping by running to the rear and taking passage to Mobile on the transports that were lying off shore, but nearly every one who was in the fort was marched off as prisoner and sent to Ship Island."[111]

Chapter 4

The Battle of Fort Blakeley

The Fight at Redoubts 5 and 6

Redoubts 5 and 6 lie to the right, or west, side of Old Blakeley Road as visitors make their way into the park heading toward the river or Battlefield Road. The current park road follows closely the route of the original Pensacola Road in this area, a route first cut during the heyday of the town of Blakeley. Redoubt 5 is located in a wooded area to the left of Skirmish Line Trail and can be accessed either by taking that trail to its intersection with Sheetz Trail (which roughly follows the path taken by the central portion of the 8th Illinois during its assault on the position on April 9, 1865) or by following the Breastworks Trail, which runs behind the position. Points of entry are located along both Old Blakeley and Battlefield Roads. The area surrounding Redoubt 6 has been opened in recent years by the park. In front of it stand monuments to the soldiers who fought in the battle and interpretive signage. On the opposite side of the road is a small field, through which Union troops charged during the battle, containing the remains of the old Blakeley town cemetery. The crosses at the edge of the field nearest the road are not graves but rather a memorial to those who fell during the Battle of Fort Blakeley. In the distance, past the park's primary tent campground, the land slopes down into a ravine that roughly divides the area fronting Redoubts 5 and 6. Altogether, it is some of the most level terrain on the battlefield.

Heading directly toward Redoubt 6 during the battle was a column of men led by the 10th Kansas, supported by men of the 27th Iowa, 117th Illinois and several companies of the 32nd Iowa. The 6th Minnesota, along with the remainder of the 32nd Iowa, stood in reserve some one thousand yards back.

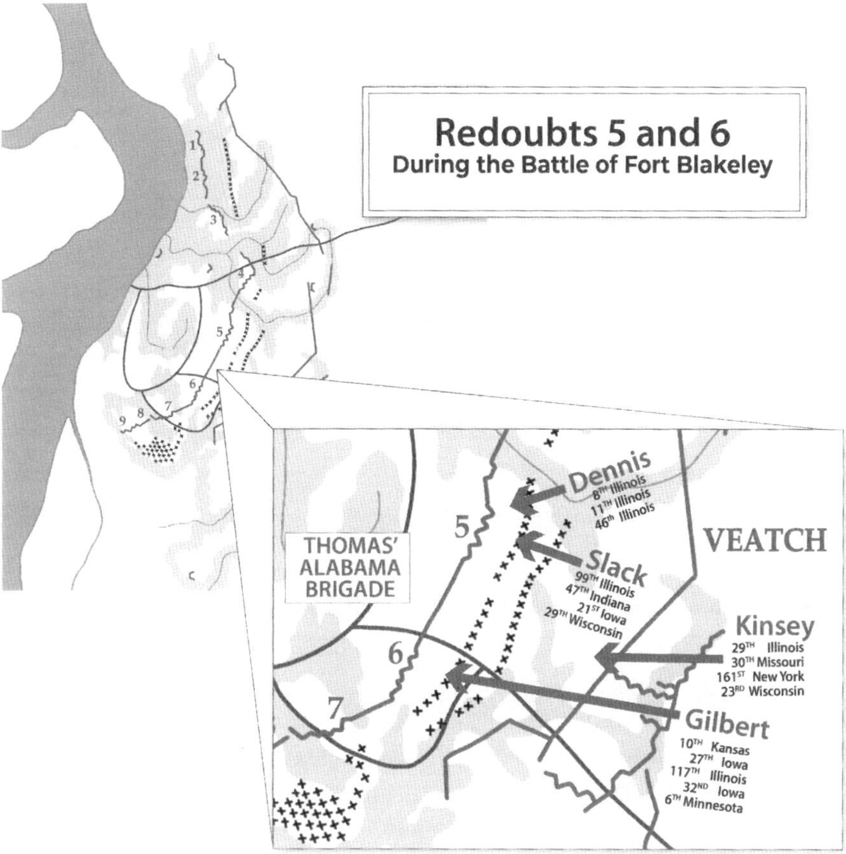

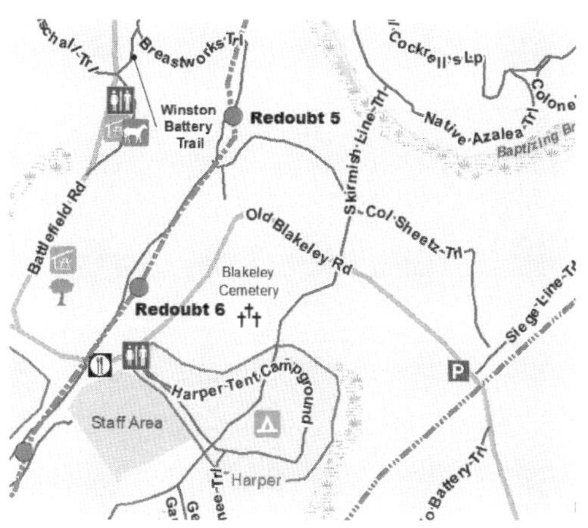

Above: Redoubts 5 and 6 during the Battle of Fort Blakeley. *Historic Blakeley State Park.*

Left: Area of Redoubts 5 and 6 today as depicted on park visitor map. *Historic Blakeley State Park.*

The leading units had about four hundred yards separating themselves and the Rebels in this sector, the majority of whom were the young, inexperienced troops of the 63rd Alabama under the command of Brigadier General Bryan M. Thomas. A scattering of artillery supported them, including ten- and thirty-pounder Parrotts, twelve-pound howitzers and a Columbiad, which, in the words of a witness, "uttered its last fierce thunders, pouring forth shell, grape, and canister" as "the musketry volleys rolled along the line in quick succession, and clouds of smoke rose up from the works." Advancing through the large swale that divided the terrain here into two relatively open plains, the attackers found themselves taking fire from their front and flank by the guns of Redoubt 5 for a short distance while they moved up to the series of obstructions placed by the Confederates. The precariousness of the position served as an impetus for them to quicken their pace, but this caused them to be funneled into a tight column directly in front of Redoubt 6 and present an easy target for Rebel gunners. The intrepid 10th Kansas, a "little band of heroes" in the words of Brigadier General James I. Gilbert, bore the brunt of the hailstorm of ordnance being hurtled against them.[112]

The Federals pressed on toward the Confederate works, crossing the Pensacola Road, and quickly scaled the parapet of Redoubt 6. Once inside Fort Blakeley, they swept the lines to the right and began rolling up the right flank of the thin gray line. All order and command broke down, and swords, revolvers, bayonets and clubbed muskets were wielded in a frenzy of fighting as, in the words of one officer, "blue and gray was all mixed together." During a few moments of disorienting confusion, some of the fort's defenders recognized their hopeless position and began to lay down their arms and surrender or gather in the corners of the redoubt with their hands up. Other individuals continued to resist with desperate ferocity. One Confederate, for example, refusing the repeated shouts demanding surrender amid the chaos, instead fired multiple successive but inaccurate shots at the officer of the 10th Kansas giving the order until a Yankee leveled him with a bullet to the head.[113]

To the right, the 8th Illinois led another grouping of Federal regiments making a beeline for Redoubt 5. Their path paralleled the park road from the point where it crosses Siege Line Trail (which runs along the third parallel of Federal entrenchments, from which the charge began) to the point where it makes a sharp bend to the left in front of a flagpole. Behind the 8th in support were the 11th Illinois on the left and the 46th Illinois on right. The 8th advanced as a broad skirmish line several hundred yards wide with its some seven hundred men "with all the compulsive force that a skirmish line can

Sketch of the area in front of Redoubts 5 and 6 as it appeared in 1866. *From* The Campaign of Mobile.

have," according to witnesses. Sweeping up to the Confederate rifle pits, it paused briefly to capture several Rebel sentries and brought its firepower to bear on the few who chose to neither surrender nor run back to the main line. It resumed the assault momentarily, with the first soldiers encountering the abatis placed by the Confederates opening holes under deadly fire for their fellow soldiers to run through. In similar fashion to the 10th Kansas, the 8th took the heaviest fire of the attackers in this sector as it moved across the gently rolling plain in full view of the Rebel guns for several hundred yards. Upon their reaching the redoubt, momentum carried them up and over the walls of the fortification, where a vicious close-quarters fight raged. Two of the first men to gain the top of the earthwork were swept away by one of the last artillery bursts from inside the redoubt. Moments later, as bluecoats poured over the walls and into the Confederate lines, the big guns fell silent as the adversaries engaged in hand-to-hand combat using rifle butts and bayonets. A number of the fort's defenders fell back into the timber line during the initial Yankee rush on their position, where they attempted to fire a ragged volley or two before the sheer numbers of the Federals were brought to bear against them. Most were surrounded and captured, with a handful making a sprint toward the river in a forlorn bid for escape from the tightening Yankee vice.[114]

In Their Own Words

2nd Division, XVI Corps

2nd Brigade

Brigadier General James I. Gilbert
"At 3 p.m. April 9, in obedience to orders from General Garrard, I moved my command to the reserve intrenched lines preparatory to charging the enemy's works….At 5:30 p.m. a rapid and severe artillery fire commenced, which was soon followed up by a general advance and charge. My main line of battle was 1,100 yards distant from the rebel fortifications; the intervening ground was covered with timber felled in every possible direction, torpedoes planted in front of the works, wire stretched from stump to stump, a double line of abates [*sic*], and in rear of all a very strong line of fortifications. At the command to advance the line raised a shout, pressed rapidly forward, reached and carried the enemy's works, and pursued the disconcerted enemy to the river-bank, capturing 9 pieces of artillery and 573 prisoners….The Tenth Kansas, a little band of heroes, rushed forward as into the jaws of death, with a determination to conquer or die."[115]

10th Kansas Volunteer Infantry
Organized at Paola, Kansas, in April 1862 through consolidation of two incomplete regiments, the 10th Kansas Infantry at first served in Indian Territory. It was sent for duty in Missouri and Arkansas afterward, participating in several skirmishes and small actions prior to the Battle of Prairie Grove in December 1862. Several of its companies were detached for service at strategic locations in and around St. Louis and Topeka in 1863. The 10th Kansas was attached to the Army of the Cumberland for the Nashville campaign, taking part in the Battle of Franklin and the Battle of Nashville in the winter of 1864. Sent to New Orleans afterward, it advanced on Blakeley and remained on duty in Alabama until August 1865.[116]

Lieutenant Colonel Charles S. Hills
"At 5:30 p.m. the movement commenced as directed. The men, leaping over our intrenchments, advanced on a run to the enemy's first line of rifle-pits, which were abandoned without much resistance, as was also his second line. While descending the slope to the ravine which lay in my front, the enemy opened with a galling fire of artillery and musketry, using shell, spherical

case, canister, and grape, which induced me to look for shelter in the ravine, in accordance with previous orders, but which, on reaching, I found to be enfiladed, and afforded no shelter whatever. For this reason no halt was ordered, our safety depending on breaking through the main works on my left if possible; if not at any point, take him on the flank and double him up.

Lieutenant Colonel Charles S. Hills. *Missouri History Museum.*

On gaining the high ground past the ravine the firing became more rapid, and had it been well directed would have been very destructive. No man in the line returned the fire, but each one devoted his whole energy to reach the works as soon as possible, climbed over fallen trees with scarce an effort, cleared each line of abatis at a single leap, and, scarcely noticing the ditch, mounted the parapets or poured through the embrasures at the recoil of the guns that their last discharge had opened for them, and their line was broken. Turning the left of my line (which after entering the embrasures had become a column) to the right, and being joined by those who had climbed the parapets, it swept down on their flank and fixed bayonets with scarcely any opposition, the men throwing down their guns and surrendering, officers waving their white handkerchiefs and delivering up their swords. Here for the first time I discovered the left of the skirmishers of the division of the Thirteenth Corps did not connect with my right, but had made an interval of some eighty yards and having a greater distance to pass over than my line had not yet reached the works. Fearing that the enemy's line in their front might, with those who had escaped from my column, discover our weakness and give us trouble, I pushed on down the line, so that the enemy might not have time to recover from his panic, and found that my right had already captured the men and guns at the center from and the infantry support on its right, most of the left having run down the ravine to the rear and for the time escaped capture. A portion of the Thirteenth Corps having now arrived, and all resistance at an end and prisoners all secure, I halted my command, reformed them, and rested the men till I received orders to join the brigade."[117]

"[I] charged their works, leaped over the parapets, and crowded through the embrasures, and either killed or captured every man in our front. Such a terrific rain of shot, shell, grape, canister and bullets I never saw…telegraph wire was stretched in every conceivable shape; and what was worse, the sand was literally filled with torpedoes; yet with all of this, we advanced with this little skirmish line into the mouths of seven heavy pieces of artillery and eight hundred muskets…works eight feet high, with a deep ditch in front filled with water.…I lost seven men killed, three mortally wounded, eight severely and three slightly wounded. No one was more exposed than I was. I leaped the works the instant that my first man did. Had a hole made through my cartridge-box, one through my pants, and two through my coat. We fought with bayonets and revolvers after we got into the works. Blue and gray was all mixed together."[118]

32nd Iowa Volunteer Infantry

The 32nd Iowa was organized at Dubuque in October 1862. Selected companies of the regiment were stationed at various points in Missouri and at Fort Pillow, Tennessee, throughout the remainder of the year. Others were assigned to service at Island No. 10. Consolidated again by the spring of 1863, the regiment took part in the Meridian campaign of early 1864, at which time certain companies were again detached and sent to Cape Girardeau, Missouri. The regiment took part in Steele's Little Rock expedition and the Red River campaign in the summer of 1864. During the winter of that year, it saw action in the Nashville campaign before being sent to New Orleans early in 1865, from which it moved on Mobile. It mustered out of service in August 1865.[119]

Colonel John Scott

"[A]bout 4 o'clock on the afternoon of April 9th the time, according to General Sheridan, when Generals Grant and Lee were seated in the house of Mr. McLean at Appomattox, completing the terms of Lee's surrender, a different scene was transpiring in the pine forest on the hill back from the Tensas. The long roll was beating, Fall in! Fall in! Every man who is able to shoulder a gun, fall in! It was for the final charge on the defense of Mobile.…Forming into line, we passed the 18th New York, Mack's Black Horse Battery…and a little farther on the 17th Ohio and 2nd Illinois. Here our brigade was halted. The 3rd Indiana battery…asked to take position at the right at the side of the 32nd Iowa. To our right was a bare knoll up in the edge of the pine timber, and exposed to full view of the rebel guns…solid shot was hurled at one of the principal rebel guns, and it was soon silenced. The artillery along our entire line then opened with renewed vigor, and the very earth for a time appeared to shake with the booming of heavy guns. Soon the order rang out along the entire line Forward! Forward! And the troops did make their way over and through that network of cheveaux de frieze and torpedoes. Charge! Charge! Was the order, as the last ditch was reached. Soon the white flag was waving over their last defenses, and in a few minutes the stars and stripes were floating there on. The last defense of Mobile was ours; the last victory won, just as the sun was sinking in the west."[120]

27TH IOWA VOLUNTEER INFANTRY

Organized at Dubuque in October 1862, the 27th Iowa took part in Steele's Arkansas Expedition and the capture of Little Rock in 1863 and was stationed in Memphis through the winter of 1863–64. It participated in the Meridian campaign of 1864 in Mississippi and then saw action in the several battles of the Red River campaign in the spring. The unit took part in several small operations in Mississippi, Arkansas, and Missouri later in 1864 prior to moving to central Tennessee and fighting in the Battle of Nashville. It moved into Alabama for the Mobile campaign from New Orleans and was stationed in Montgomery after the fall of Blakeley until July 1865.[121]

Private Cyrus E. Smith

"On Sunday, afternoon, April 9, a few minutes before we made the charge on the fort, an Indiana battery that belonged to our brigade…fired three shells at the big gun and disabled it, so that when we crossed our third line of works we were not molested by the gun. There were torpedoes planted in the open spaces, and as they were all marked with a stick and a piece of white paper, I had no trouble in avoiding them. There were two wires stretched along about a foot from the ground, and as I saw a soldier to my right trip on one of these I jumped over them, and came to an abatis of tree tops about eight feet high—the outer limbs all sharpened. I climbed the obstruction, and a few rods farther on came to a second abatis, prepared like the first and about 10 rods from the rebel line of works. Just as I reached the top of this last abatis Albert Tennis caught a bullet on the finger, and at the same time a Sergeant of Co. B was shot in the face. When I got within four rods of the works a Johnny stuck his gun over the works, then raised his head to look over. I was looking for something of this kind and got the drop on him before he could fire, and he dropped behind the works. I went up to the works, and, shoving my gun over the edge, looked over for him. He yelled: 'Don't shoot!'"[122]

National flag carried by the 27th Iowa Volunteer Infantry. *State Historical Museum of Iowa, Des Moines.*

Unknown Soldier, 27th Iowa Infantry

"At 2 P.M. on the 9th of April we received orders to be ready to make an assault on the Fort at 5 P.M. Soon everything was in readiness and a deathlike stillness prevailed along our whole line. Not a shot was fired and all seemed to be nerving themselves for the coming charge. The hours of suspense before a battle are much more trying to the soldier and tests his courage more than the actual participation of it, for then he has time to think soberly and candidly of the danger he is to encounter....The ground that we had to advance over was made nearly impassible as the ingenuity of the enemy could make it. It was covered with heavy growth of pine trees, which had all been fallen with the tops out so that it seemed impossible to get through them. Then there were two lines of abatis and chevaux-de-frise, while between the abatis and chevaux-de-frise were two lines of wire stretched about eight inches from the ground for the purpose of tripping us so that we would fall and impale ourselves on the sharp points of the chevaux-de-frise as we advanced. At 5:30 P.M. our artillery opened with a heavy fire which did considerable damage to the enemy's works, besides disabling several pieces of artillery. At precisely 6 P.M. the order came to advance and firmly, steadily, we moved forward as fast as we could run, and without firing a shot. In five minutes after the order was given to advance, our Division commanded by Maj. Gen. Garrard, was inside the rebel entrenchments with loaded guns and bayonets fixed and the Confederate garrison were at our mercy."[123]

117th Illinois Infantry Regiment

The 117th Illinois organized in Springfield in September 1862. It served primarily in and around Memphis until December 1863, when a detachment was sent in pursuit of General Nathan Bedford Forrest's cavalry. It joined General William T. Sherman's forces for participation in the Meridian campaign in the spring of 1864, from there being sent to Louisiana, where it saw action in the Red River campaign. In the summer of 1864, the unit was engaged in minor actions in northern Mississippi and Missouri. The 117th fought at the Battle of Nashville in December 1864 before being sent for duty in New Orleans in early 1865. After fighting at Blakeley, it assisted in occupying Mobile and ended the war in Montgomery in August 1865.[124]

Regimental flag of the 117th Illinois Infantry. *Illinois State Military Museum, Springfield.*

Colonel Risdon M. Moore.
Missouri History Museum.

Colonel Risdon M. Moore
"In less than ten minutes after the command 'forward' was given the regiment swept over half a mile of dense abates [*sic*] and a line of very formidable earth-works, in which were at least eleven guns bearing on the line."[125]

Private Otto Wolf
"[W]e received orders to get ready to go out on the skirmish line by 6 p.m. with two meals of rations and what bedding they wanted to take along with them. The boys only took along a rubber blanket. We were out on the picket line by 6 p.m. and were ordered to charge. Our skirmish line was about one half a mile from the Rebel fortifications. The Rebs had cut down all the trees in front of the Breastworks and sharpened all the limbs so that it was nearly impossible to get over them besides having two lines of abattis [*sic*] all around the fort. Well, our regiment charged over it all in about fifteen minutes.... Our brigade captured about eight hundred prisoners. Our regiment took a small camp color....I have just got a pot of beans on the fire that need tending so I will close for the time."[126]

Lieutenant Colonel Jonathan Merriam
"When the signal to advance was given the men sprang out of the trenches and rushed forward with cheers such as the 16th Corps only can give, at full speed.

The ground was terrible to charge over, covered with thickly tangled fallen timber and broken with marshes and swamps which it was almost impossible to get through....The rebels poured a terrific fire upon us both with artillery and musketry, grape and canister. Shot and shell came like hail but there was no faltering....Soon the works were reached, the cheveaux-de-frise and the thickly sown torpedoes passed and the grandly thrilling cheers of victory rang out as we halted for a half moment upon the Rebel battlements to unfurl our banners and reform our lines. The fight was over but we plunge into the thick undergrowth to gather up the fleeing, terror-stricken rebels. At last, utterly exhausted and breathless, we halt. The work is done."[127]

6th Minnesota Volunteer Infantry

The Sixth Minnesota Volunteer Infantry was organized in 1862. It served in the Dakota War, a conflict between the United States and several bands of

Regimental flag of the 6th Minnesota Volunteer Infantry. *Minnesota Historical Society.*

Dakota Sioux Indians that flared up in southwestern Minnesota in the late summer of 1862, and then remained on duty in that region until the summer 1864. The unit was sent to Helena, Arkansas, at that time and from there to St. Louis and New Orleans before being assigned to Canby's command for the Mobile campaign. It saw its first action against Confederate troops at Blakeley. The 6th ended the war in Montgomery in the summer of 1865.[128]

Private Alfred J. Hill. *From* History of Company E, of the Sixth Minnesota Regiment of Volunteer Infantry.

Private Alfred J. Hill

"About 5:15 p.m. the various batteries of the Union forces opened fire upon the enemy's lines, but their guns did not reply for about ten minutes, when the cannonading became brisk on both sides, lasting until 25 minutes to 6; the battery near the regiment sharing in it. Now it ceased suddenly on our side, and in its place were heard the ringing cheers of the soldiers as they rose, in full view of the reserves, from their trenches in the front and rushed towards the Confederate fortifications. By 6 o'clock the noise of the cannon had ceased and a white flag was visible, which told of the enemy's surrender; and shortly the Stars and Stripes superseded it."[129]

1ST DIVISION, XIII ARMY CORPS

Brigadier General James C. Veatch

"At 5 p.m. of the 9th instant I received an official note from Capt. J.F. Lacey, of General Steele's staff, saying that the entire skirmish line in front of Blakeley would advance at 5:30 p.m., and that Major-General Steele wished me to advance and enter the enemy's works if possible. My division occupied one brigade front of the line of investment, the left extending a few rods south of the road leading from Sibley's Mills to Blakeley, and joining Garrard's right, extending to and joining General Andrews' left. I immediately placed the Second Brigade, Brigadier-General Dennis, on the front line, and brought up the Third Brigade, Lieutenant-Colonel Kinsey, One hundred and sixty-first New York, commanding, to support it. The First Brigade, Brigadier-General Slack, was held in reserve. A section of the Seventh Massachusetts Battery, Captain Storer, was all the artillery I had in position. After a very sharp artillery fire from our line the forward movement commenced. The Eighth Illinois Infantry, Colonel Sheetz, advanced as skirmishers, followed by the Forty-sixth Illinois Infantry, Colonel Dornblaser, on the right, and the Eleventh Illinois, Colonel Coates, on the left. The enemy's main works were about 600 yards from our skirmish line. His skirmishers were well advanced and covered by a strong line of rifle-pits. As the Eighth Illinois advanced it received a very hot fire from the skirmish line, but with shouts and cheers it pressed forward over the rough ground and obstructions of fallen timber, captured rebel skirmishers, and pressed forward through the double line of abatis to the enemy's main work. A rebel battery on the right of the Sibley road fired canister with great rapidity as the line approached. The right of the line reached this battery, and instantly mounting through the embrasures, its four guns were silenced and captured. The whole regiment dashed over the works led by their gallant officers, and captured 300 prisoners, and pressing forward were the first troops that reached the landing. The Eleventh and Forty-sixth Illinois quickly followed, and were halted and formed inside the works. The whole brigade deserves the highest credit for the splendid manner in which the charge was executed. No regiment could have done better than the Eighth Illinois. It was among the first, if not the very first, to plant its colors on the rebel works. My command captured 300 prisoners, two Parrott guns, two 12-pounder howitzers, one 8-inch columbiad, and 500 stand of small-arms, a large amount of ammunition and ordnance stores, all of which were left on the ground when the command was ordered back to camp at 12 o'clock at night."[130]

Brigadier General James R. Slack

"Sunday, April 9th, remained in camp all day recuperating from the effects of the forty-eight hours' excessive fatigue through which the command had just passed. At 5:30 p.m. an assault was made upon the rebel fortifications by our whole line and their works carried most gallantly, and the last work manned by the rebels for the defense of Mobile taken possession of by the Federal army."[131]

Brigadier General James R. Slack. *From* History of Huntington County, Indiana.

Regimental flag of 29th Wisconsin.
Wisconsin Veterans Museum (Madison).

29TH WISCONSIN VOLUNTEER INFANTRY REGIMENT

The 29th Wisconsin Infantry was organized in Madison in September 1862. The unit served at various points in Illinois and Arkansas prior to participating in the several battles of the Vicksburg campaign in 1863 and taking part in the Red River campaign in 1864. After the Mobile campaign, it was mustered out of service at Shreveport in June 1865.[132]

1ST DIVISION, XIII CORPS
2ND BRIGADE

Brigadier General Elias S. Dennis

"In the afternoon of that day (April 9) I was notified by the general commanding the division that our lines would be advanced, and an effort made to carry by assault the works in our front, 5 p.m. being the hour named. At 5 p.m. my command was moved to the front….My instructions to Colonel Sheetz, commanding the Eighth, were, that as soon as the lines on his flanks commenced moving he should move forward with them, the Eleventh and Forty-Sixth Illinois would follow at a proper distance. At the hour named the advance commenced handsomely under a galling fire of artillery from the enemy's batteries, and after gaining about half the distance were received by a withering fire of musketry from the enemy's infantry concealed behind his works. In front of and running parallel with the works were several lines of abatis, and a wire was also stretched a few inches from the ground for the purpose of tripping the men; yet, notwithstanding all these obstacles, the troops pressed onward, and in less than five minutes from the time of starting the Eighth Illinois Infantry was scaling the works and going through the embrasures, some minutes before the troops, either on the right or left, had reached them. They captured at this point quite a number of prisoners, one battle flag, one thirty pounder and one twenty pound Parrott gun, and two twelve-pound brass howitzers in position; also one seven-inch gun which had not yet been mounted."[133]

8TH Illinois Infantry

The 8th Illinois was organized in October 1861 at Cairo. It took part in the capture of Fort Donelson in early 1862 prior to fighting in the Battle of Shiloh and participating in the Siege of Corinth. The 8th took part in the entirety of operations against Vicksburg in 1863 and remained on duty there until the summer of 1864. It moved to Memphis afterward, being sent to New Orleans in January 1865 and from there to join forces for the advance on Mobile. It helped occupy Mobile after the fall of Blakeley, remaining on duty at posts in Louisiana and Texas until the spring of 1866.[134]

Colonel Josiah A. Sheetz

"In about five minutes after the charge commenced my line ascended the parapet of the enemy's works, capturing the four pieces of artillery and quite a number of infantry. The advance of my line, which was somewhat irregular from the difficult nature of the ground, entered the enemy's works at least two minutes before the troops upon my right or left effected a lodgement. Lt. Col. Lloyd Wheaton and Sgt. John M. Switzer, Company B, entering the embrasure of the 30 pounder, were the first of my command to enter the enemy's works. As soon as my command had carried the works in my front I reformed my line, throwing skirmishers forward to the river bank, and soon after, under instructions from Brigadier-General Dennis, I marched my command to the landing at the river, taking possession of three 9-inch guns, two Coehorn mortars, a number of arm chests full of muskets, many thousand rounds of ammunition for small arms, and a magazine containing a vast quantity of ammunition for heavy guns. Much property, consisting of mules, wagons, tents &c. was also captured."[135]

46TH Illinois Infantry

The 46th Illinois organized at Camp Butler in December 1861. It took part in operations against Forts Henry and Donelson early in 1862 prior to seeing action at the Battle of Shiloh and the Siege of Corinth. It served in northern Mississippi for most of the remainder of 1862 and into 1863 before participation in the Vicksburg campaign. The 46th took part in several minor actions in Mississippi, Louisiana and Tennessee afterward. In February 1865, it arrived in New Orleans as part of forces assembled for the campaign against

Regimental flag of the 46th Illinois Infantry. *Illinois State Military Museum, Springfield.*

Mobile. It served at several posts in Louisiana after the fall of Blakeley, being mustered out of service in January 1866 at Baton Rouge.[136]

First Sergeant Bela St. John

"Got a mail this p.m. and also got orders to be ready to go into the pits at 6 o'clock this evening. A little later we were ordered to fall in immediately and were moved out to one of the ravines in the rear of our line where we stacked arms and the 11th took position on our left and directly after a battery came into position on the left of the 11th and opened on the rebels. The 8th Illinois was in the pits in front of us. Soon after the battery opened our regt. moved off some distance to the right and went into the pits that were used for the reserve. By the time we got into the pits the artillery on both sides was blazing away very fast and the skirmishers were moving forward. On the right we could hear loud yelling and on looking we could see our skirmishers all along running forward and on the right of us we could see the main line moving forward. Just then the order for us to move forward so we jumped out of the works as best we could, yelling like good fellows and started on the run. The yelling was so loud that we could not hear the report of the artillery. The brush and fallen timber was so thick we could keep no line but run on like a lot of boys after a rabbit. Just after we got outside our works we had to go down through a deep ravine filled with fallen timber. We got across it by running on logs and jumping from one to the other. By the time we got up the hill on the other side the firing had about ceased in front of us and we heard the order to halt but I do not know as it was given by the Colonel. Anyhow we stopped and were forming the company when we noticed the colors were going on and was some distance ahead so Capt. Marsh again gave the order to forward and off we started as fast as we could run. I passed close to two dead and several wounded of the skirmishers from the 8th Illinois. I asked two different ones if they were wounded and they said yes but to go on and do all I could and not mind them. All at once several boys that were in front of me fell heavily on their faces and as I came up I see they had fallen over a wire which was stretched along about a foot from the ground. I did not see it in time so but I fell partly over myself. Passed over another wire and through several lines of brush pickets, abatis, but as I happened to be in a path I got through without hindrance. The Color Sgt. (Tom Joiner) mounted a fort where two guns were and struck the colors on the top and as we came up we went over and formed a line inside. As I came over the works I see that there was a lot of Johnnies in the fort where the works were higher so they would be safer from our fire. One of their guns was dismounted. Four guns were in the works which our regt. covered and a huge siege piece lay a few rods inside in the road that had not been mounted yet. Close to it was its carriage which had been struck with a shot and one of its wheels smashed. After the regt. had formed we moved just outside the works and stacked arms to rest a little."[137]

11TH ILLINOIS INFANTRY REGIMENT

The 11th Illinois was mustered into service in July 1861 at Cairo. The unit saw significant action at the Battle of Fort Donelson, where more than half of those in its ranks suffered casualties. It fought at the Battle of Shiloh and in the Vicksburg campaign prior to being sent on expeditions to Natchez and Yazoo City. The regiment served in Tennessee, Arkansas and Louisiana afterward before moving from the New Orleans area to Alabama for participation in the Mobile campaign. It ended the war in Baton Rouge.[138]

Private Thomas Fisher
"Charged the reb works and took them at sun down. This evening never was so tired of running and hollering in my life.…We made our first charge right over trees, bushes, dead and wounded of ours and rebs. Took lots of prisoners."[139]

Private Thomas Fisher. *Illinois Civil War Project, https://civilwar.illinoisgenweb.org.*

Lieutenant George D. Carrington
"I saw to the left our men on top of the works firing down while the flashes from the inside were aimed up. While these men were yet on top of a redoubt a Rebel fired a cannon almost under where they were standing. This was the last cannon shot fired from their intrenchments. As we jumped down inside they were 'throwing down their hot Enfields.'… One Rebel Captain came swearing he would never surrender to a 'damned Yankee.' One of the boys raised his musket and fired, the bullet passing through his brain and down he went in a pile. Poor fellow! He might have lived. It was all done so quick no one could interfere."[140]

Colonel James. H. Coates
"On the afternoon of April 9 received orders to move up the works and to support the Eighth Illinois Infantry (who were the skirmish line of the brigade front) on the left, with orders that when the reserve of General Garrard's line advanced for me to also advance. Consequently at about 6 p.m. the whole line advanced, my regiment being within supporting distance of the line of the 8th Illinois Infantry…and advancing in line of battle, and in this formation reached the works of the enemy, where, upon orders, I halted and stacked arms, remaining there for about an hour, when the regiment advanced through the timber to the river to pick up prisoners trying to escape."[141]

Chapter 5

The Battle of Fort Blakeley

The Fight at Redoubts 7, 8, and 9

Redoubts 7, 8 and 9 anchored the right flank of the Confederate line at Blakeley. The relatively closely spaced fortifications defined the portion of the earthworks, which made a sharp turn south, toward the Tensaw River, after the broad arc away from the waterway in their central sector. The terrain in which these redoubts are situated is as varied as any location along the line. Redoubt 7 fronts a short plain; in the distance a gently sloping ravine is located between another patch of level ground. Behind it lay even more even terrain. Much of this area had recently been under cultivation as a corn field at the time of the battle. Redoubts 8 and 9 are perched on bluffs with ravines on either side and behind and front narrow swaths of flat ground that, to the right, makes a steady descent into a valley through which a multi-channel stream flows. A narrow swath of relatively flat land fronted Redoubt 9, which had recently been planted in corn, but much of it had been filled with fallen trees and other debris by the Confederates. Period maps indicate that much less timber had been felled in front of the Confederate lines in this sector, the broken areas of old corn fields and debris-filled rough terrain supplying the fields of fire engineers desired and the steep ravines and swampy terrain ahead and to the side of the earthworks effectively funneling any attack into the narrow passable space they defended.

Directly behind Redoubt 8 and behind and to the right of Redoubt 9, the southernmost position along the Confederate line, lay a thick tangle of underbrush growing in a boggy riverside swamp.

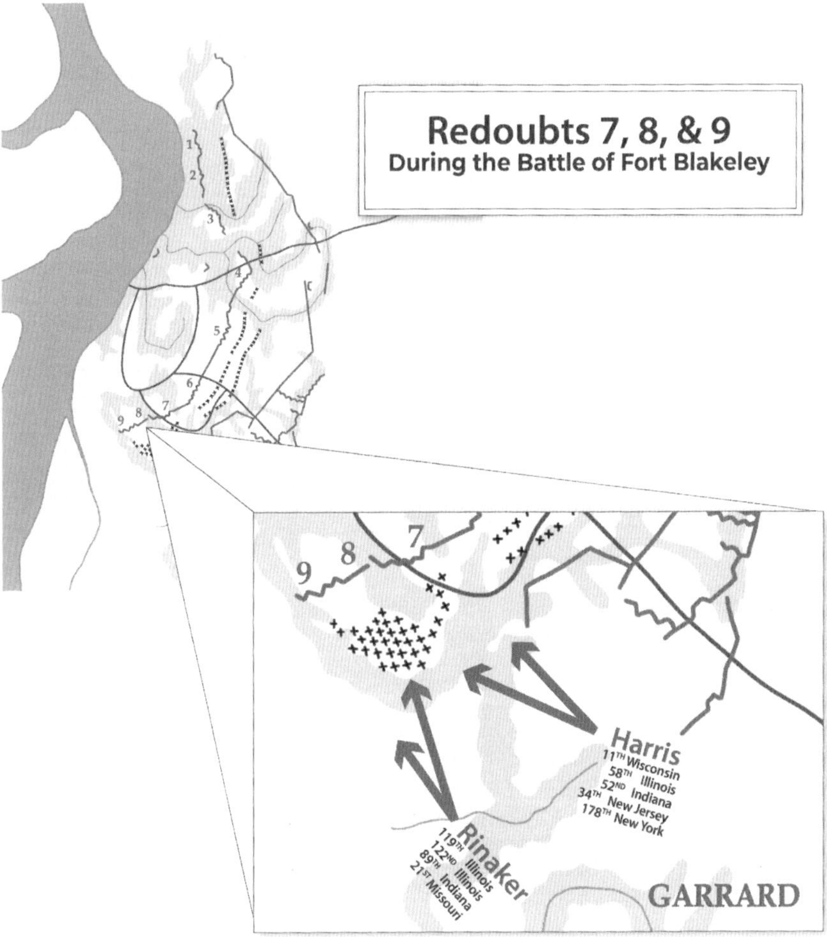

Redoubts 7, 8, & 9
During the Battle of Fort Blakeley

Harris
11TH Wisconsin
58TH Illinois
52ND Indiana
34TH New Jersey
178TH New York

Rinaker
119TH Illinois
122ND Illinois
89TH Indiana
21ST Missouri

GARRARD

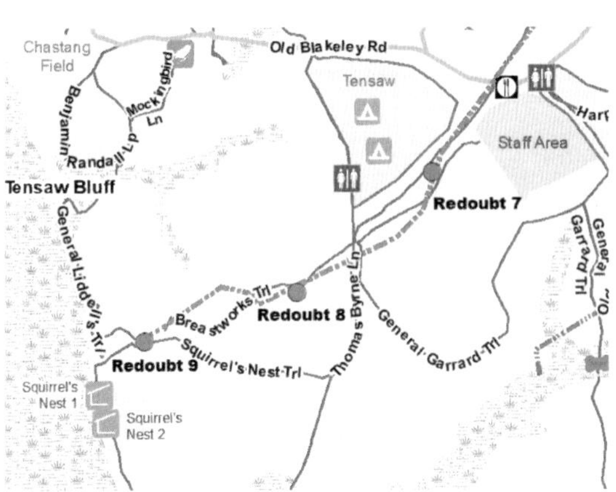

Above: Redoubts 7, 8 and 9 during the Battle of Fort Blakeley. *Historic Blakeley State Park.*

Left: Area of Redoubts 7, 8 and 9 today as depicted on park visitor map. *Historic Blakeley State Park.*

Behind the earthworks along this section were the young boys—and a few older men—of Thomas's Alabama Brigade. Very few had seen any previous military action. Most had been rushed into service in recent months as the Confederacy made a desperate attempt to put every able-bodied man it could into its army. Officers had questions about their reliability in battle. General Liddell had noted in correspondence to General Cockrell that he believed the experienced Missourians to Thomas's left were "the only ones here that can be relied upon thoroughly" and had directed at the onset of the siege that Thomas take pains to impress upon his troops "the importance of holding their position to the last, and with the determination never to surrender." Records are unclear exactly which units provided artillery support in this sector, but Winston's Battery, with its Parrott rifles and twelve-pounder howitzers, is believed to have been positioned in Redoubts 7 and 8, while Culpepper's Battery, a unit of the Palmetto Battalion from South Carolina, had its guns in Redoubt 9. Advancing against them during the battle would be an equally mixed Federal grouping of veteran midwestern units that had fought in several major clashes of the war, most recently at Nashville, along with the only Missouri unit wearing blue on the battlefield (the 21st) and the only New Jersey (34th) infantry unit. They would form on the extreme left of the Federal lines, in an area with less substantial trenchwork than the heavier, defined earthworks to their right.[142]

The area is accessed by visitors today by traversing the Breastworks Trail, a hiking trail that runs along the entirety of the Confederate line in the park and crosses Old Blakeley Road just west of Redoubt 6. The trail ends at Redoubt 9, on the bluff overlooking the swampy terrain connecting with the Tensaw River and the park camping shelters known as the "Squirrel's Nests." It is perhaps the most difficult area of the park from which to appreciate that a major battle once raged on the spot, being a peaceful and wooded area with little clearing.

Had you been standing on the bluff occupied by Redoubt 9 on April 9, 1865, and scanning the rolling terrain to the left, back toward Redoubt 7, at 5:45 p.m., you would have been able to catch glimpses of the advancing Federal column as it emerged from the wood line and rushed across the relatively narrow open space on the extreme Confederate right toward Thomas's "Boy Brigade." The 58th Illinois, 11th Wisconsin and 178th New York were in the van of a group of at least five regiments targeting the area between Redoubts 7 and 8, with a second line of troops rushing to their support. Directly in front of you, clawing their way up a debris-strewn ridge in the distance and crowding into the narrow stretch of open land

Monument at the grave of Lieutenant Joshua L. Moses at Mobile's Magnolia Cemetery. *Historic Blakeley State Park.*

straight ahead, came another group of attackers led by the 119th Illinois. To the extreme right, the 21st Missouri formed the left flank of the Federal column, its light-blue regimental flag discernable among the several national flags studding the front line of the mass of blue-clad men rushing through thick debris toward the Confederates. The Missourians were adjoined by the 122nd Illinois and the 89th Indiana in this sector of the charge, covering one of the shortest but most debris-riddled distances to be traversed by the attackers anywhere on the field.

To their credit, Thomas's men met them like veteran troops and stood their ground as best they could during an intense, short-lived firefight. The skirmishers in the advanced rifle pits laid down a murderous fire at the oncoming bluecoats, momentarily causing some doubt of the issue in this sector as "the ranks of the leading groups were visibly thinned." "Young as they were, they fought like devils," remembered one Federal who attacked Thomas's line. The skirmish line at last broke and ran toward the main entrenchments, where an even stiffer resistance awaited. Troops fell dead on the parapet in the close-quarters affair. In one of these isolated melees, for example, a band of about a dozen graycoats rushed down on the lead elements of the 11th Wisconsin, where they encountered the line between Redoubts 7 and 8 with shouts of "no quarter to the damned Yankees," shooting down all who came within range. Lieutenant Angus McDonald somehow survived to tell the tale of the fight here, despite being shot and struck by several bayonets. He was on the ground, using a fallen Rebel as a shield against another blow, when Sergeant Daniel Moore shot his assailant, earning himself a Medal of Honor for the rescue later. Some of the artillerymen in this sector, notably the men of the Palmetto Battalion, attempted to keep firing until the bitter end. Reputedly, Lieutenant Joshua L. Moses, likely the last officer of the Confederate garrison to fall and the last Jewish commander of Rebel forces to perish in the war, continued the struggle until he and some of his gunners were surrounded and shot down at their posts after firing some of the final shots of the battle.[143]

Four Medals of Honor were later awarded for the capture of battle flags in this vicinity: John H. Callahan of the 122nd Illinois and Samuel McConnell, George F. Rebmann and John Whitmore of the 119th Illinois. In addition to the aforementioned Sergeant Moore, a medal was also awarded to Charles M. Rockefeller of the 178th New York for a daring reconnaissance of the Rebel line in the area of Redoubt 7 immediately prior to the battle.[144]

IN THEIR OWN WORDS

Union Lines

XVI Corps
2nd Division

Brigadier General Kenner Garrard
"On the 9th instant, the morning after the capture of Spanish Fort, General A.J. Smith, commanding corps, visited my headquarters and instructed me to assault Fort Blakeley at the earliest practicable moment, and for that purpose he would order up to my assistance McArthur and Carr, and all the artillery I wanted....During the morning I placed in position on my extreme left, to guard my lines from the fire of gun-boats, Hendricks' and Cox's batteries, of the First Indiana Heavy Artillery, consisting of 30-pounders. Three of these pieces were turned on the enemy's line until 5 p.m. when they ceased by my orders. At 3 p.m. on my extreme right I placed in position behind my rifle-pits Mack's Black Horse Battery of six 20-pounders, with orders not to fire except when the enemy opened...that I wanted my lines in their advance protected....Similar orders were given to the other batteries under my command, viz, Rice's 17th Ohio (four Napoleans), Lowell's 2nd Illinois (four 10-pounder Parrotts), and Ginn's 3rd Indiana (four 10-pounder Parrotts). At 2 pm I sent for my brigade commanders...and gave them the following orders....I directed them to move their commands into the trenches, placing one half in the rifle pits of the skirmishers and one half in those of the reserves. That at 5:30 pm a single line of skirmishers should advance, and as soon as it appeared that they were advancing with success that a second line of skirmishers should follow, and when the first line reached the enemy's works then the main line should charge. I was induced to adopt this plan owing to the terrible obstructions in my front and to avoid loss of life....As the right of Rinaker's and left of Harris' lines were the most advanced, I ordered that at this point the attack should commence and be taken up to the right and left as rapidly as possible....At the appointed

Brigadier General Kenner Garrard. *From* Harper's Weekly, *February 11, 1865.*

time, under a brisk fire from all of the artillery, the first line moved, then the second, then the artillery ceased firing, and I saw our men on the enemy's works. I immediately ordered a cheer and a charge. This cheer was taken up on the right of my division, and as I advanced in the charge I looked to the right and saw our whole army in front of Blakeley most gallantly taking up my movement. My division carried the enemy's works."[145]

119TH ILLINOIS INFANTRY

The 119th Illinois organized at Quincy in September 1862. Its first assignment was to guard the Mobile and Ohio Railroad, a vital communication link. It was stationed at Columbus, Kentucky, and at various points in Tennessee until January 1864, when it joined Sherman for his Meridian campaign. Afterward, it fought in the entirety of the Red River campaign, taking part in several battles and helping construct the famous dam on the Red River at Alexandria that was designed by Lieutenant Colonel Joseph Bailey and allowed imperiled Union gunboats to escape being trapped by low water. The 119th afterward fought against Forrest at the Battle of Tupelo and other engagements in northern Mississippi before a short stay in Missouri. The unit fought at the Battle of Nashville and then was sent to New Orleans, where forces were being gathered for the Mobile campaign. Following the

National flag carried by the 119th Illinois Infantry. *Illinois State Military Museum, Springfield.*

fall of Fort Blakeley, the 119th moved to Montgomery for a brief stay. It mustered out of service in Mobile in August 1865.[146]

Colonel Thomas J. Kinney

"[A]t 5:30 pm., everything being ready and the charge about to commence, I discovered that the rebel skirmish line had anticipated our movements and broke from their rifle-pits in great disorder. This, in my judgment, being the appropriate time for prompt action, I ordered my skirmishers to charge the works. As a cloud, we raised from the rifle pits and with a shout and cheer onward we went. At this juncture the enemy opened with artillery from all the guns they could bring to bear on us, but it only had the effect of hurrying on their own destruction. Onward we went, over fallen trees, ravines, etc.…until the main line of his works was reached, sweeping everything before us…we were compelled to shoot down several of their artillerists, who continued to work their guns upon our advancing lines after we had occupied the forts."[147]

Private Lewis H. Potts

"The morning of April 9th saw the Union line in position for a siege.… Garrard's strategy was to first assault the fort with a heavy skirmish line the size of a regiment to determine the enemy's strength. Only once this was determined was a full assault to begin.…In other words, one regiment was to act as the turkey in a turkey shoot to see how many were shooting! These orders were issued to brigade commander John I. Rinaker, who in turn selected the turkey: the 119th Illinois Volunteer Infantry. A light rain fell that morning. The 119th targeted redoubts 8 and 9 on the Confederate right. As the weather cleared, the First Indiana Heavy Artillery began pounding the redoubts from Blakeley Bluff behind the men. The weather worsened, and the time for a charge drew near. The existing skirmishers returned to their units and the 119th took their place in the front at mid afternoon. Thirty minutes before the charge was to commence, at 5 p.m., all artillery fell silent. Colonel Kinney stood to the far left of the 119th as it prepared for the assault. He noticed, however, that the Rebel skirmishers had seen the Union's heavy skirmish lines and were retreating in disorder. The confusion thus created was not an opportunity lost on Kinney. The buglers sounded 'forward', and the charge began.…The turkeys turned into vultures. Within 10 minutes they were over the works of Blakeley. The fighting continued as the 119th found itself 'compelled to shoot down several of their artillerists, who continued to work their guns upon our advancing lines.' By the end of the hour the 119th had taken 10 cannons, two mortars, several rebel officers and scores of enlisted men. Among the regiment's prisoners was CSA Gen. Lidell himself, along with the colors of three of the units under his command."[148]

Captain Samuel McConnell

"[W]e advanced against the fort, the bullets and shells mowing down our companions with merciless precision. My clothing was cut in several places by bullets, and when I reached the breastworks I had only one man of my company, Private Wagner, with me.... At the point where we reached the breastworks was an angle containing three large guns, which were dealing out death at an alarming rate, and making the atmosphere so smoky that we could see for only a short distance.... We were so close to the muzzles of the guns that when they were discharged the air pressure thus created knocked us back into the ditch. But we immediately sprang up and managed to climb over the works before the rebels could reload. Seeing us come over the breastwork, the gunners turned and fled, and some surrendered, leaving us in undisputed possession."[149]

Captain Samuel McConnell. *From* Deeds of Valor: How America's Heroes Won the Medal of Honor.

First Sergeant Lemuel Burke

"At 5 PM Col. Kinney came to us and told us that assault was to be made on the rebel works about 400 yards to our front. The 119th formed in one rank, the even numbers to fire and odd numbers to leap out the skirmish ditch and charge at a given signal. The 119th was to form the skirmish line to cover the whole front of our Brigade...at the signal given the skirmishers leaped out the ditch and advanced on a run toward the rebel works, coming upon the rebel skirmishers in their pits that could make no defense, and surrendered. The whole line advanced rapidly under a heavy fire of grape and canister and musketry, over a deep marsh hollow, the ground being covered with fallen timber, brush, 3 lines of abatis torpedoes and telegraph wires. Many of us were thrown down over the wires, I among the rest. I saw many men skulking behind logs and stumps that I thought ought to have been closer up and should be getting closer up to support the front. I was among the reserved of the skirmishers that stayed in the ditch until the main line came up, and consequently was not among the first men that went over the works, but I think I was about 30 steps behind. Just as I was near the breastworks one piece of their 3 pieces of artillery was fired at us and it looked like it came out of the ground almost, while at the same time I could see our men firing down from the top of the breastworks at the rebels and the Johnnies were firing up at our men. By the time I got into the works resistance on that part of the line had ceased, one of the gunners having been shot with the match in his hand in trying to fire his piece, and another with the rammer in his hands after having refused to surrender—and so with many others at the gun. But the infantry soon gave up for after piercing their line we turned to the left and after a few shots enfilading them they threw down their arms and surrendered…

After the troops of the 13 AC saw that we were charging on the left they took it up and the charge was made along the entire line….During our march in from the battlefield the woods resounded with the wild cheers—I never saw men so alarmed as were the prisoners. Many of them cried and begged for life. Many of them were mere boys and some were gray headed old men. The officers were generally pretty good looking men."[150]

21st Missouri Volunteer Infantry

The 21st Missouri Infantry was organized in February 1862 and saw its first action at the Battle of Shiloh. It moved from there to take part in the Siege of Corinth and participated in the fighting there and at Iuka in the fall of 1862. The regiment served at various posts in Kentucky and Tennessee until early 1864, when it took part in the Meridian campaign. The unit fought in the battles of the Red River campaign and afterward in the Battle of Nashville. The 21st moved from New Orleans into Alabama for the Mobile campaign. After the fall of Blakeley, it was stationed at Mobile and at other points in Alabama until being mustered out of service in April 1866.[151]

Flag of the 21st Missouri Volunteer Infantry. *Missouri State Museum, Missouri State Parks.*

Brevet Major M.D. McAlester
"It [the 21st Missouri] took part in the many skirmishes in the approach and siege of Fort Blakely and lost several men killed and wounded on the 9th of April....In the capture of that place two of the color-bearers were killed, but the colors were successfully planted on the works before that of any of the many others that were fully as anxious as the Twenty-first to have their flag first. The loss of the regiment was about equal to that of the whole brigade, it being on the extreme left of the army, which was not equal to the front of the enemy's works, causing a cross-fire of artillery and musketry to be given it from the enemy's right."[152]

Captain Edward K. Blackburn
"April 10, 1865
Thomas H. Roseberry. Sir.

Dear Sir,
It becomes my painful duty to inform you and your family that your son Matthias is no more. He was mortally wounded while with his company Charging the Rebel Fort Blakely [*sic*] on the evening of the 9th at 5 o'clock P.M. and died the 10th at 3 o'clock A.M. his Brother Rees and Hughes stayed with him from the time he was wounded until his death. His private Accts I will leave with his brother to settle up and forward as you may direct. His Final Statement I will forward to Washington D.C. as soon as possible. He has pay due him from the 31st day of October 1864 also $240.00 net Bounty. The action was short and bloody. I lost seven men in killed and wounded. Sergeant Woodruff and Chas. B. Lewis are both wounded. I remain with feelings of Sympathy for you in your loss.

Yours respectfully
ED. K. BLACKBURN, CAPT.
Co. G 21st Mo. Vet. Vols. I"[153]

122ND ILLINOIS VOLUNTEER INFANTRY
The 122nd Illinois organized in Carlinville, Illinois, in August 1862. It served at posts in Kentucky, Tennessee, Mississippi and Alabama throughout 1862 and 1863, participating in several small actions with cavalry threatening railroad connections. In July 1864, it saw heavy action at the Battle of Tupelo, being stationed in and around Memphis before and after the battle. The 122nd joined forces in pursuit of General Sterling Price's Rebel army

in the fall of 1864 before being ordered to Nashville, where it fought on December 15 and 16. The unit arrived in New Orleans in February 1865 and moved into Alabama for the campaign against Mobile the next month. The regiment mustered out of service in Mobile in July 1865.[154]

Colonel John I. Rinaker

"On the 9th, about 3 p.m., the general commanding ordered the brigade to be moved into position to support the advance of a strong skirmish line, which was to feel of the enemy's strength of forces and works, to move the skirmishers forward at 5:30 p.m. I thereupon ordered Col. T.J. Kinney, 119th Illinois Infantry, to be ready to move his regiment forward to the skirmish line, relieving the skirmishers then on duty, and to put the whole of his regiment into the advance rifle pits. After he had examined the ground his regiment was put into the advance line about 5 p.m. The relieved skirmishes were ordered to join their regiments, and ammunition was brought forward to the advanced reserve line for distribution. As Col. Kinney's regiment moved into the rifle pits beyond the creek, the 89th Indiana, under Lt. Col. Hervey Craven, and 21st Missouri Veteran Volunteer Infantry, under Capt. Charles W. Tracy, were moved forward in line of battle just in Kinney's rear to the creek, which is about thirty yards in rear of the rifle pits, on the left not so far. The 122nd Illinois, under Lt. Col. James F. Drish, was formed in reserve opposite to and about 100 yards in rear of the center. Anticipating that it was necessary, in order to save my skirmish line in the advance…as soon as Colonel Kinney's line was ready I ordered the 122nd Illinois to move forward and overlap the 89th Indiana and 21st Missouri, and to move straight forward as the line advanced, following Colonel Kinney's center, and to fill up the space between the 89th Indiana and 21st Missouri, as these two regiments separated to the right and left, the 89th connecting with Colonel Harris and the 21st Missouri supporting the extreme left of the skirmish line. This line was formed tolerably well under cover and within 250 yards of the rebel works. I then went forward to the rifle pits to see when Colonel Kinney was ready to start and to superintend the general movement of my command. Colonel Kinney was on the extreme right of his skirmish line. I was at this

Colonel John I. Rinaker. *From* History of Macoupin County, Illinois.

time notified by Major Healy, of General Garrard's staff, that all was ready and waiting for me to start. About the same time an artillery officer (Captain Ginn) reported to me that he had some guns with which he was to report to me, but had not found me till that moment. He told me where his guns were, and I asked what he could do with them there; could he do execution with them? He replied that he could. I told him to open on the enemy's works on my left, which he did promptly, and, I am happy to state, with effect. In a moment the rebel skirmishers commenced running. Colonel Kinney started his line rapidly forward; his reserves were ordered out to support his skirmishers, and the buglers sounded 'forward.' I at once put the whole line out on double-quick, knowing that under the artillery fire of grape and canister which was opened on my skirmish line it must either be destroyed or go into the fort; and from that moment the whole brigade was, with a shout, going over the fallen trees, tangled vines and brush, and through the swamp at a full run, and that under severe and rapid fire from artillery and musketry. In from five to ten minutes from the advance of the skirmish line the enemy's works were carried and the national flag waved over them. The regiments were reformed in the fort as soon as possible after entering it, and the trophies and wounded which belonged to the command looked after and taken care of."[155]

Lieutenant Colonel James F. Drish
"Once more I hasten to inform you of my safety—after having met the foe in battle....In the evening about 4 o'clock while we were digging rifle pits word came that our lines were to advance on the enemy's at 5 PM....The wild scene which followed cannot be depicted. Imagine a space a quarter mile wide covered by a dense pine forest all shaped and falled with tops toward us besides three lines of brush abatis...all protected by works some 8 feet high with port holes to shoot through. When the order to charge was given every man went on his own hook. No such thing as keeping lines.... The Rebel infantry left the works or surrendered as soon as we got to them, but the artillery men fought to the last some of them choosing to be shot down sooner than stop shooting their pieces."[156]

Private William H. Peter
"[T]he Johnnies wonder how we ever got to the fort. I believe some of them think there is something supernatural about us, and say that when we start it seems like nothing can stop us....Col. Drish was wounded in shoulder soon after starting. Jas. Pinckard was shot in the right arm, since amputated near

the shoulder, poor boy I feel so sorry for him....Several of the boys were knocked down by shells bursting so near them. One had the rim of his hat all torn off behind a piece of shell....The prisoners say if we had waited till the next day we would not have found a man there as they were going to evacuate....The next thing will be to surround Mobile and take it. That will finish off the business in this part of Rebeldom."[157]

89TH INDIANA INFANTRY

The 89th Indiana was organized at Wabash and Indianapolis in August 1862. The regiment had its first assignment in Kentucky, where it had the misfortune of being surrendered to General Braxton Bragg at Munfordville in September. After being paroled, the unit was sent for duty at posts in Memphis and northern Mississippi, where it skirmished with forces under General Forrest on several occasions. It participated in the Meridian campaign and the Red River campaign, during which it was in the thickest part of the fighting in several actions. It was among the Federal units sent in pursuit of Price's Confederate army in 1864 prior to fighting in the Battle of Nashville in December. The regiment moved from Dauphin Island in the spring of 1865 for the advance on the defenses of Mobile. Following the fall of Fort Blakeley, the 89th was on duty at Montgomery and Mobile before being mustered out of service in July 1865.[158]

Lieutenant Colonel Hervey Craven

"On the morning of the 9th, I received orders to have the regiment in readiness to move at a moments warning, and at 4:30 PM we were ordered out, arriving at the reserve of the skirmish line at about 5 o'clock. The 89th Ind. took position on the right of the brigade, with orders to cross a small branch of water, take position at the skirmish line, at the brow of the hill, there to remain in readiness to support Col. Thos. J. Kinney's regiment, the 119th Illinois....The 89th were taking position in the entrenchments formerly prepared by the skirmish line, when an incessant fire of artillery from our own and the enemy's batteries, and our own skirmishers becoming suddenly engaged in our front, all because inspired with enthusiasm, and in obedience to orders, moved forward yelling, and charging the enemy's works

Lieutenant Colonel Hervey Craven. *From* History of Madison County, Indiana.

and entering them, the particulars of which I am unable to give, for owing to the immence [*sic*] amount of fallen timber with which the ground was covered, it was impossible to ride."[159]

58TH ILLINOIS INFANTRY

Organized at Chicago in February 1862, the 58th took part in the capture of Fort Donelson and occupied Fort Henry before participating in the Battle of Shiloh, where many of its number were captured. Detachments participated in action at Corinth and Iuka and in guarding prisoners at Camp Butler, Illinois, throughout the remainder of 1862 and into summer of 1863. Others were detailed to garrison duty at locations elsewhere in Illinois and Kentucky. The regiment fought in the Red River campaign and the Tupelo Expedition of July 1864, in addition to several smaller actions in Arkansas and Missouri. It took part in the Battle of Nashville, afterward being sent to New Orleans; from there it advanced into Alabama for the Mobile campaign in the spring of 1865. It remained on duty after the capture of Mobile until April 1866.[160]

Captain John Murphy

"We had only just time enough to assume our position when a general advance was ordered. The battalion mounted the works with a yell, and rapidly as the nature of the ground would permit advanced to the enemy's position. Regular lines could not be maintained, as for the greater portion of the ground over which we charged was utterly impassable, but there was no skulking in this battalion. Every officer and man reached the rebel works, most of them entering the fort before the guns to our right and left had been silenced."[161]

178TH NEW YORK INFANTRY

The 178th New York traced its origins to the consolidation of several units at Staten Island in June 1863. It mustered into service later that year, at first being stationed in Washington, D.C., as a provost guard. It was sent to Mississippi in the fall of 1863, where it took part in Sherman's Meridian campaign in the spring of 1864. It fought in several engagements during the Red River campaign afterward, going from there to posts in Arkansas, Tennessee, Mississippi and Missouri before joining Canby's force for the campaign against Mobile. It mustered out of service at Montgomery in April 1866.[162]

Lieutenant Colonel John R. Gandolfo

"On the afternoon of the 9th I received orders to advance upon the enemy's works, being connected on the right by the Fifty-eighth Illinois Infantry and

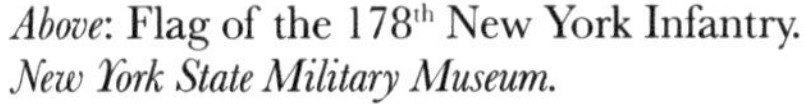
Above: Flag of the 178th New York Infantry. *New York State Military Museum.*

Right: Lieutenant Colonel John R. Gandolfo. *Missouri Historical Society.*

the left by the Eleventh Wisconsin Veteran Volunteer Infantry. On arriving on the line of skirmishers I ordered my regiment to charge rapidly and not halt until the enemy's works were in our possession. The rapidity of the advance was greatly impeded by fallen timber, and although exposed to a galling fire of grape and canister on each flank, as well as musketry in front, I gained the breast-works of the enemy with trifling loss, and planting my colors, the first upon their works, I pushed on to the river after those of the enemy who had fled in that direction and occupied a small earth-work on the right, leaving the prisoners in the rear to be cared for by the supporting column."[163]

11TH WISCONSIN INFANTRY

The 11th Wisconsin Infantry was organized at Camp Randall in Madison and mustered into service in October 1862. It served at posts in Missouri and Arkansas prior seeing action in the major battles of the Vicksburg campaign and participating in the Siege of Jackson. The unit pursued General Nathan Bedford Forrest's cavalry in northern Mississippi and western Tennessee in 1864. It was stationed in Texas afterward before joining forces gathered for the movement against Mobile. After the Battle of Fort Blakeley, it occupied Mobile and was mustered out of service there in September 1865.[164]

Left: Regimental flag of 11th Wisconsin. *Wisconsin Veterans Museum (Madison, WI).*

Right: Major Jesse S. Miller. *Wisconsin Veterans Museum (Madison, WI).*

Major Jesse S. Miller
"April 9 received orders to move out to advance rifle-pits and form on the left of One hundred and seventy-eighth New York Volunteers and Fifty-eighth Illinois, preparatory to assaulting the enemy's works. Companies A, F, and D were deployed as skirmishers in advance of the pit, and were ordered to lie down. At 5:30 the order was given to move forward, when the regiment rushed from their concealment with a yell and made for the enemy's works in its front under a murderous fire, mounted the parapets, and carried them at the point of the bayonet, capturing over 300 prisoners, 2 guns, and several horses and mules. The loss of the Eleventh in this charge was 15 killed and 48 wounded, of which 1 second lieutenant was killed and 2 first lieutenants wounded."[165]

Colonel Charles L. Harris
"[D]uring the afternoon of the 9th I was sent for by the general commanding Second Division, and there met General Gilbert and Colonel Rinaker…and General Veatch…and it was then decided that this division should move on the enemy's works in two lines, with a strong line of skirmishers in advance at 5:30 pm on the following order: First Brigade, Third Brigade, Second Brigade, with Veatch's division on our right as a support. At 5 pm I moved my brigade into our works, putting the 11th Wisconsin, 178th New York, and Battalion 58th Illinois in the front line, with the 34th New Jersey as the second

line. At 5:45 o'clock I received an order from Brigadier-General Garrard to advance my skirmish line…and I immediately after started my first line, which moved as rapidly as the nature of the ground would admit, it being covered with fallen timber and two lines of abatis over a distance of 450 yards on the left and 600 yards on the right, and although exposed to a galling fire of grape, canister, and musketry on the left flank and front, my first line soon reached and carried the enemy's works. The 11th Wisconsin having the shortest distance to go, first entered their works, and fighting hand to hand succeeded in breaking their lines…the 178th New York and 58th Illinois following close up, rendering good service. When the first line got near the enemy's works the second line was ordered to move forward, which they did without loss."[166]

34th New Jersey Infantry

The 34th New Jersey Infantry began organization at Beverly, New Jersey, in September 1863. Stationed at various points in Mississippi, Tennessee and Kentucky, the unit took part in several minor actions throughout 1864. It was sent to New Orleans early in 1865, joining forces concentrating for the movement against Mobile shortly afterward. After the Battle of Fort Blakeley, the unit served at Montevallo, Talladega, Gainesville, Tuscaloosa and other points in Alabama until mustered out of service in April 1866.[167]

Colonel William Hudson Lawrence

"April 9, still engaged on saps, having completed the redoubt last night at 5:30 p.m. Formed 5:45, our first line of battle driving all before them. The reserve was ordered to charge, which they did in gallant style. Our loss during the day was 2 killed, 1 wounded, and 1 missing. Returned to camp at 8 p.m., Blakely having been gloriously captured."[168]

52nd Indiana Infantry

The 52nd Indiana Infantry was organized at Rushville and Indianapolis in February 1862. In its first time in the field, it saw action at Fort Donelson and helped garrison Fort Henry. It participated in the Siege of Corinth in April and May 1862, afterward being stationed in the Memphis area. The unit operated in a number of smaller actions in Tennessee and Arkansas until being sent on the Meridian campaign of early 1864. The 52nd took part in the Red River campaign later that year and afterward fought at the Battle of Nashville. It moved to New Orleans in February 1865, from which it departed for the Mobile campaign. Following the fall of Fort

Left: Regimental flag of the 34th New Jersey Infantry. *New Jersey State Capitol Joint Management Commission/New Jersey State Museum.*

Right: Flag of the 52nd Indiana Infantry. *Indiana War Memorial.*

Blakeley and Mobile, the unit moved to Montgomery and then Tuskegee. It mustered out of service in September 1865.[169]

Lieutenant Colonel Zalmon S. Main

"On the afternoon of the 9th instant I was ordered by the colonel commanding the Third Brigade to move the 52nd Indiana from camp to the reserve line of the picket and form on the left of the 34th NJ; that the 34th NJ and 52nd Indiana would form the third assaulting line of the Third Brigade, and the assault would be made by a line advancing from the advance picket-line at 5:30 p.m. At about this time, or a little later in the day, the advance line moved forward, at which time the colonel commanding the brigade gave the order for a general attack upon the enemy's works. As soon as this order was communicated to my regiment they sprang over the works with a determination and with a seeming eagerness that but few troops exhibit under similar circumstances. Every officer and man in the regiment, so far as I know, used every exertion to reach the enemy's works as soon as possible, to assist in its capture; and although it was not possible for the regiment to be the first over the enemy's works, as the distance was so much farther for them to go than it was for some, yet it arrived in time to capture twenty seven prisoners of war, including one captain and one lieutenant."[170]

Confederate Lines

Redoubts 7, 8 and 9

62ND Alabama Infantry

The 62nd Alabama was organized at Mobile in March 1865 by combining Lockhart's Battalion—which had joined Confederate service at Selma in 1864 and fought at the Battle of Chehaw Station and at Fort Gaines before being captured there in August—with several companies of recent conscripts. Troops from the 62nd were originally placed in the lines at Spanish Fort until relieved by Holtzclaw's Brigade and sent to Fort Blakeley. It served there throughout the remainder of the siege of Blakeley and fought in the battle of April 9, after which the great majority of those in its ranks were captured and sent to prison on Ship Island, Mississippi.[171]

Private Asa M. Piper

"On the 9th day of April the U.S. troops charged our thin line with Negroes first, and we slaughtered them fast, some 2,000 being killed in a few minutes with ground torpedoes in the ground and by shot and shell from the breastworks. Then we were charged by five lines of battle and captured on the evening of the 9th."[172]

Left: Flag of the 62nd Alabama Infantry. *Alabama Department of Archives and History.*

Right: Brigadier General St. John Richardson Lidell. *Library of Congress.*

Brigadier General St. John Richardson Lidell
"Toward evening of April 9th, Negro troops under Steele assaulted our left, next to the river, but were driven back with heavy loss. Later the enemy fire heavily increased from all the batteries, and the discharges were incessant. Just at sunset they suddenly ceased, and the plain around our front swarmed with assaulting lines. The enemy scrambled over brush, abatis, stretched wires, through subterra explosions, added to our fire of grape, canister, and musketry. It was well and quickly done. The works were entered. Some of my men were shot from the rear, while at their guns firing to the front. Thus Blakeley fell at the point of the bayonet. No flag was ever lowered. Some men escaped by swimming to the gunboats, some on rafts hastily improvised, some through the marshes; many were drowned, and many killed or wounded."[173]

Private James Thomas Jefferson Watson
"[W]e were sent to Blakeley where we built good breast works in a week when General Canby came on us with 40,000 Yankee soldiers. There were 4,000 of us boys. The Yankees manifested great surprise that we were so few. They said we killed 4,000 of them. Of course, they captured us all, with the Bay on one side and the Yankee army on the other."[174]

Chapter 6

The Last Moments of the Battle at the Blakeley Waterfront

The town of Blakeley, for which Fort Blakeley was named, had once been one of the largest cities in Alabama. By the time of the Civil War, though, it ranked as little more than a village. Founded by speculator Josiah Blakeley and incorporated in 1814, the town stood along a narrow elevated riverfront plain on the banks of the Tensaw River. At first, Blakeley had developed rapidly as it strove to be a commercial rival to Mobile. Easily accessible by water or by land—it was the terminus of major regional roads running north to Stockton to join the old Federal Road and east all the way to Pensacola—by the early 1820s the town could claim a population of perhaps two thousand people. Dozens of homes could be found clustered within the town and dotting the surrounding landscape; more than two dozen well-stocked stores flanked its busy dirt streets; two of the finest hotels in the region welcomed its many guests; and a biweekly newspaper, among the first in the state, kept citizens up to date on current events. Two of the first steamboats to be built and used in Alabama were constructed along its waterfront, whose extensive wharf system welcomed ships from ports ranging from New England to the West Indies. The town served as the seat of government for Baldwin County and was even designated an official United States port of entry.[175]

By the time of the construction of Fort Blakeley in 1864, however, the town had been virtually abandoned, owing to a series of setbacks that stalled the town's growth. Recurring outbreaks of yellow fever in the 1820s had carried off an alarming number of citizens and scared much of the

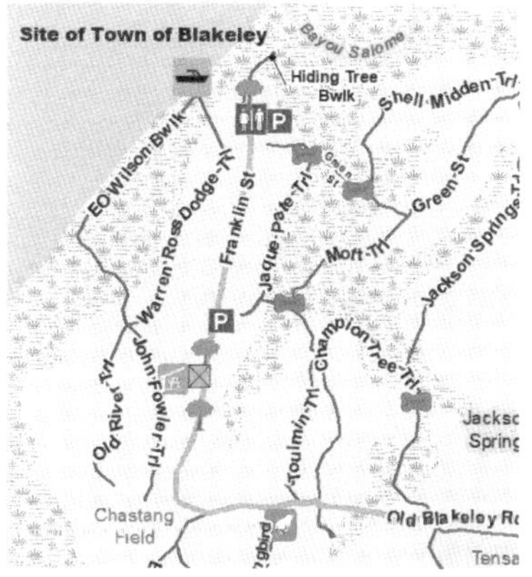

Left: Area of Blakeley town site as depicted on park visitor map. *Historic Blakeley State Park.*

Below: This section of the map of the defenses of Blakeley, produced by Nicola Marschall, shows what remained of the town of Blakeley at the time of the battle. The area depicted stretches from modern-day Chastang Field at right, down what is now called Franklin Street, to the park dock at left. A hotel is noted as still standing near the landing, while several other buildings, possibly both commercial and residential, are shown. The structure labeled "C.H." at center-right is the courthouse. *National Archives.*

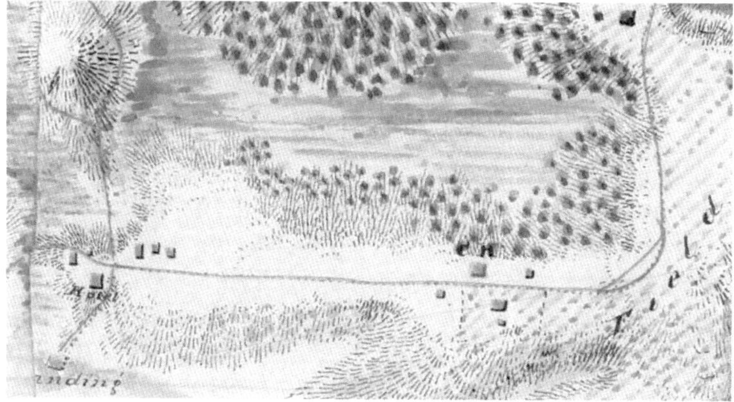

remainder into moving to what they perceived to be healthier locations. Plus, real estate prices had skyrocketed at the time of the town's heyday, and with no shortage of land available in the area, many potential investors began to look elsewhere. In addition, Mobile had taken notice of its upstart competition for shipping traffic and had begun to take steps to increase the ease of access to its harbor at the expense of other regional ports such as Blakeley. As residents of the once-thriving town left for other opportunities, Blakeley gradually receded back into the wilderness. The courthouse remained in the town, and it would serve as the county seat through the end of war and beyond. By the time the Confederate army arrived in Blakeley, however, it was a virtual ghost town. It was the strategic location along the deep and wide Tensaw, not its importance as a population center, that made it militarily significant.

Confederate authorities availed themselves of the long-shuttered port facilities at Blakeley and took advantage of any remaining intact structures still standing in the town as they stockpiled supplies for the growing garrison in old Blakeley's downtown. A number of Confederate marines, many of them paroled after capture while on Rebel boats during the Battle of Mobile Bay, worked along the riverfront unloading the supplies for the troops who manned the lines at Fort Blakeley. Any Confederate officials visiting the site from Mobile, the administrative center for the district, would have arrived at the Blakeley dock. The small Confederate naval squadron assigned to coordinate with the army in defense of the position, including especially the ironclad CSS *Nashville* and the wooden sidewheel gunboat CSS *Morgan*, which made several visits to Blakeley and shelled Federal lines, would have been regular sights along the Blakeley waterfront. As the siege of Fort Blakeley progressed, the townsite hosted a field hospital where the wounded could be treated immediately.

Following are a few accounts of the chaotic last moments of the Battle of Fort Blakeley at the waterfront, describing the scene there as the Confederate line surrounding the old townsite was overrun and small groups of soldiers rushed pell-mell for the river in a desperate bid to escape. Fleeing soldiers took up boards from docks or simply jumped into the river in a forlorn attempt to evade capture. Many were shot down in the effort, and an unknown number were persuaded to return to shore at gunpoint. The CSS *Nashville*, lying nearby at the time of the battle, moved in toward shore and attempted to rescue all the Rebel soldiers it could before moving back to Mobile. A handful of survivors somehow made it away. The exact number is unknown but is believed to be just a few dozen. Today, the story of those frantic last moments are remembered at the "Hiding Tree," a large live oak with a hollow base where, legend holds, Confederate soldiers hid in a bid to escape capture by Federals. Whatever the veracity of the tale, it reminds us of the frenzied final moments of the fall of Fort Blakeley.

In Their Own Words

Lieutenant George Warren

"We saw in a moment 'the jig was up.'…Our first thought was 'escape.' All of us instinctively rushed to the wharf, a half mile distant, hoping that when we reached the river some means of escaping capture would be found there. When I got to the wharf I sprang immediately on board a flatboat lying there, which was heavily loaded with some sort of freight. Captain

Young, General Cockrell's aide-de-campe, and 30 or 40 men followed. We shouted to those on the bank to 'cut loose,' but not a man would lend a hand. I sprang into the water up to my waist, and with a very dull knife cut a hawser as large as my wrist—in just half the time it would take me to do it again. I was dragged aboard by one of the men, wet up to my neck. After we started to move off on the flowing tide and current, some one on shore shouted, 'The boat is loaded with powder, and the enemy will fire into you and blow you up.' This created a little panic and half a dozen jumped overboard, thinking to swim ashore. One I know, probably more, was drowned. We instantly threw off the tarpaulin and in a few minutes had relieved our boat of a hundred cases of artillery powder. Just as we were leaving shore, Captain Maupin and 5 or 6 other officers pushed out in a small skiff, but they had proceeded but a few yards, when their boat sank with them and left the whole party floundering in the water. I learned afterwards that none of them were drowned. Numbers of men took planks that were lying on the wharf, and throwing them into the water, stretched themselves on one end and struck out for—where? Certainly, they didn't know, for it is fifteen miles across the bay to Mobile, and could not expect to reach that point by such slow locomotion. Many of them paddled out to the sand-bars, where there was growth of cane to hide in, but the returning tide brought several additional feet of water, which drove them out from their retreat. Our 'Flat' had floated several hundred yards away from shore, and the tide and current were bearing us rapidly away, when the enemy first came into sight. For a while they were so engaged in receiving the surrender of our friends on shore they did not notice us. This gave us an opportunity of witnessing that humiliating scene. We saw Colonel McCown put his white linen pocket handkerchief on the end of a ram-rod, step in front of his little squad of men, and waving this emblem of submission, surrender the Third and Fifth regiments of infantry. Other officers did the same."[176]

Quartermaster Alden McLellan

"About this time I was at the field hospital, being detained by the surgeon in charge (I forget his name) to assist in amputating the leg of a wounded man, which I was required to hold above the knee. The delay was prolonged because of the time it took to get the man under the influence of chloroform. As soon as I was relieved the hospital steward and I made a run for a wharf to get planks to escape upon, I throwing down four planks. The steward took two, and I ran off on them. By this time the Federals were on the bluffs of the river, about two hundred yards off, and were firing at every object in the river.

Some of the shots struck quite near me. I concluded not to take a plank ride just then, and was busy fastening a twenty-dollar gold piece in the lining of my cap when a Federal called out 'Say, you fellow with a green shirt on, come up or you will get hulled next time.' I obeyed, making my way to the bluff where others of our men were. In a short while a Federal corporal with one man took another officer and me and started for the rear. When we got to the works, there were several explosions. Some of the incoming victorious troops had got up on the subterra shells that we had placed in front of the works and were more or less injured. They talked very ugly towards us, so our guard had us sit down a little on one side until the troops passed. On our way to the rear we stopped at a wagon train, and our guard got us some coffee and crackers. While there a Federal abused us for being Rebels, etc. Our guard told him to stop; but he did not until the guard gave him a slap, which rolled him over, and told him to go off and attend his mules. We were then taken to where the other prisoners were bivouacked for the night. The next morning we started for Greenwood, on the east shore of Mobile Bay. After going about three miles, we were countermarched into the abandoned Spanish Fort, which was under fire of one of our batteries in the marsh toward Mobile.…The next day were shipped by transport to Ship Island."[177]

Major Robert S. Bevier

"The gunwale of our boat was oak, and by lying flat on the bottom we were safe. The bullets splashing in the water around us. Our craft was struck often, but none of its occupants were touched. They shot at us as long as we were in range, and even after we had passed beyond it. One enterprising Yankee, I am sure, must have strained his gun in his effort to reach us. His balls came skimming along the water and sunk under their own weight a few yards off. We at last passed beyond their reach, even with artillery, and as the current was carrying us into the channel that led around under the guns of Spanish Fort, we concluded to cast anchor and trust to the chances of being picked up by friendly boats."[178]

Major Robert S. Bevier. *From* History of the First and Second Missouri Confederate Brigades, 1861–1865.

Lieutenant John Bennett, CSS Nashville

"April 9, after seeing the garrison safely removed from the eastern bank of the river, which was effected before daylight, the *Nashville* was anchored

Sketch of the CSS *Nashville. Alabama Department of Archives and History.*

off Blakeley in the entrance of Tensas, where she remained during the day waiting for ammunition....From 5:30–6:30 pm, a continuous discharge of artillery and small arms, mingled with loud cheers, was heard along the whole line of intrenchments. A few minutes before this a request from General Liddell was brought me by Lieutenant Commanding Myers that I would anchor the ship at a point in the Blakeley River he indicated and open upon the enemy's right. This could not be complied with because of the current at that point and the absence of holding ground, and also for the reason that I should much endanger the men of our extreme left....As soon as I discovered the enemy gaining upon our position, as indicated by the firing and cheering, I moved the ship close to the Blakeley shore and rescued such of the garrison as were able to float themselves off. Learning from one of the refugees that General Liddell was on the beach seeking to escape, I dispatched the gig under command of Passed Midshipman Carroll to the point indicated, but unhappily, before the boat could reach the shore the enemy's sharpshooters were at the water."[179]

William Lochiel Cameron

"[T]he Yanks and Rebs were so mixed up that the vessels dared not fire their guns. And then there came with a rush our poor fellows, closely followed by the enemy. Our men jumped into the water. Many could not swim, and those who could were an easy mark for the negro soldiers, who fired at them from the bank and at us in the boats. We picked up all we could and quickly retired to our respective vessels, where we landed them and returned for more. I do not know how many were rescued; but many were drowned, some killed in the water and some on the shore, and the rest surrendered."[180]

Private C.W. Gerard

"Col. Spurling of 2nd Maine Cavalry was among first to enter works, went on down to landing at Blakeley. On the way to which he captured a mule, all saddled and bridled. Mounting, he road down and found a rebel gunboat just leaving the wharf. The Captain was on deck, and Colonel Spurling, raising his carbine to his shoulder, ordered the Captain to surrender. Seeing this persuasive instrument leveled at his head, in the hands of a man who is a notorious deadshot, the Captain said 'I surrender.' 'Come ashore, then.' 'I will, sir.' And the Captain started down the gangway, as the Colonel supposed, for his small boat, but when he got down where he was safe, ordered steam to be put on, and got away. It was a very novel idea, that, however, one man ordering a gunboat to surrender."[181]

Charles B. Johnson

"Passing into Blakeley early this morning after it surrendered at 5 PM yesterday, an opportunity was given me to see things pretty much as the Confederates left them. One thing that interested me greatly was some captured haversacks containing Johnny's rations. The meat was such that our men would never have tasted unless reduced to the verge of starvation, and the bread seemed indescribably poor, and of such character as a Northern farmer would hardly feed to his hogs. It seemed to have been made from meal of which was more than half was bran, and after being made into small pones—dodgers—had been apparently cooked in the ashes and given about the appearance that two or three day's sun-drying would bestow. That men would consent to live on such food, and with scarcely any pay, daily encounter the vicissitudes of army life, and, when occasion called, cheerfully risk their lives in battle, is a high tribute to Southern hardihood, pluck, and courage."[182]

Epilogue

THE BATTLEFIELD TODAY

Historic Blakeley State Park is a cultural and natural heritage park encompassing more than 2,100 acres of the largest National Register site in the eastern United States. Open 7 days a week, 365 days a year, it offers an extensive trail system that can be utilized by hikers, bikers and horseback riders; RV, tent and horse trailer camping facilities; camping shelters and cabins; a robust series of educational programs and guided tours; and year-round access into the Mobile-Tensaw Delta via its fifty-passenger pontoon boat, the *Delta Explorer*. It is one of the largest and most diverse attractions in the Gulf Coast region.

The park is committed to the preservation and interpretation of its Civil War battlefield. With one of the best-preserved concentrations of intact Confederate and Union earthworks in the nation, the park contains more than two-thirds of the nearly three-mile-long Confederate line and nearly ten miles Union works in three parallels. The majority of these are incorporated into our growing trail system, which provides access to these unique cultural heritage assets. Plans call for additional trails providing easy access to the entirety of the earthworks at Blakeley. Visitors may explore the battlefield on their own with this guide, a smaller printed brochure highlighting a few of the key focal points, a cellphone tour or by scheduling a guided tour. The park also offers a special "The Civil War On the Eastern Shore" cruise along the Tensaw on occasion, which allows visitors to see portions of the battlefields at Blakeley and Spanish Fort and learn about the campaign for Mobile as it played out on both land and water.

Aerial images of Redoubt 4 on the battlefield at Blakeley. *Tim Ard.*

Brian Kelso.

Reconstruction of Confederate defenses in front of Redoubt 4 in the park today. *Historic Blakeley State Park.*

Blakeley's natural beauty belies the fact that it was once the scene of a pivotal battle waged for control of the city of Mobile and access to Alabama's strategic river systems. The serenity of its shady wilderness trails and rolling meadows, the peaceful murmuring of its streams and the gently lapping waves along the banks of the mighty Tensaw today all make it difficult to imagine in the mind's eye what the place looked and sounded like as nearly twenty thousand men waged a desperate struggle over the course of nine days in April 1865. Simultaneously, this tranquil natural setting renders the effort even more poignant, for it is a place where men fought and died, where they performed daring acts of bravery that echo through the ages and where they perished in sudden acts of violence with their stories untold. It is one of the Gulf Coast's foremost connections to a national cataclysm that altered the course of our nation's history. It is hallowed ground.

Order of Battle

Battle of Fort Blakeley

Confederate Forces

Confederate District of the Gulf
Major General Dabney H. Maury
Commanding Headquarters, Mobile

Eastern Division, District of the Gulf
Brigadier General St. John Richardson Liddell
Commanding Headquarters, Blakeley

French's Division
Brigadier General Francis M. Cockrell

Missouri Brigade	**Mississippi Brigade**	**Alabama Brigade**
Colonel Elijah Gates	Colonel T.N. Adair	Brigadier General Bryan Thomas
1st and 4th Missouri	4th Mississippi	62nd Alabama
2nd and 6th Missouri	7th Mississippi	63rd Alabama
3rd and 5th Missouri	35th Mississippi	
1st and 3rd Missouri Cavalry	36th Mississippi	
(dismounted)	39th Mississippi	
	46th Mississippi	

Artillery
Captain John B. Grayson
1st Alabama Artillery
Tarrant's Alabama Battery
Winston's Tennessee Battery
1st Mississippi Artillery
1st Missouri Battery
Battery C, South Carolina Palmetto Battalion

Union Order of Battle

Army of West Mississippi

Major General E.R.S. Canby
Major General Frederick Steele

1st Division

United States Colored Troops
Brigadier General John P. Hawkins

1st Brigade	2nd Brigade	3rd Brigade
Brigadier General William A. Pile	Colonel Hiram Scofield	Colonel Charles W. Drew
73rd USCT	47th USCT	48th USCT
82nd USCT	50th USCT	68th USCT
86th USCT	51st USCT	76th USCT

2nd Division, XIII Corps

Brigadier General Christopher C. Andrews

2nd Brigade	3rd Brigade	Artillery
Colonel William T. Spicely	Colonel Frederick Moore	Connecticut Light, 2nd Battery
76th Illinois	37th Illinois	Massachusetts Light, 15th Battery

97th Illinois	20th Iowa
24th Indiana	34th Iowa
69th Indiana	83rd Ohio
	114th Ohio

1ST DIVISION, XIII CORPS
Brigadier General James C. Veatch

1st Brigade	**2nd Brigade**	**3rd Brigade**
Brigadier General James R. Slack	Brigadier General Elias Dennis	Lieutenant Colonel William B. Kinsey
99th Illinois	8th Illinois	29th Illinois
47th Indiana	11th Illinois	30th Missouri
21st Iowa	46th Illinois	161st New York
29th Wisconsin		23rd Wisconsin

SECOND DIVISION, XVI CORPS
Brigadier General Kenner Garrard

1st Brigade	**2nd Brigade**	**3rd Brigade**
Lieutenant Colonel John I Rinaker	Brigadier General J.I. Gilbert	Colonel Charles L. Harris
119th Illinois	117th Illinois	58th Illinois
122nd Illinois	27th Iowa	52nd Indiana
89th Indiana	32nd Iowa	34th New Jersey
21st Missouri	10th Kansas	178th New York
	6th Minnesota	11th Wisconsin

Notes

Chapter 1

1. The campaign for Mobile is chronicled in a number of excellent books. Sources consulted for this study include Buel and Johnson, *Battles and Leaders of the Civil War*, vol. 4, *Retreat with Honor*; Andrews, *History of the Campaign of Mobile*; Bergeron, *Confederate Mobile*; Blount, *Besieged*; Brueske, *Last Siege*; Gottschalk, *In Deadly Earnest*; Hansen and Nicolson, *Siege of Blakeley and the Campaign of Mobile*; Hearn, *Mobile Bay and the Mobile Campaign*; Hughes, *Liddell's Record*; Jordan, *Operational Art and the Campaigns for Mobile*; Noles, "Confederate Twilight," 28–37; O'Brien, *Mobile, 1865*; Trudeau, *Out of the Storm*; U.S. War Department, *War of the Rebellion: A Compilation of the Official Records of the Union and Confederate Armies* (hereafter *OR*); and Waugh, *Last Stand at Mobile*.
2. Bergeron, *Confederate Mobile*, 37, 41, 156; O'Brien, *Mobile, 1865*, 15; Blount, *Besieged*, 29; Andrews, *History of the Campaign of Mobile*, 31; Farragut, *Life of David Glasgow Farragut*, 469.
3. Bergeron, *Confederate Mobile*, 43, 176; O'Brien, *Mobile, 1865*, 32; Brueske, *Last Siege*, 32–35; Blount, *Besieged*, 31–35; *OR*, part I, vol. 49, 875.
4. The best source of information on the development of the defenses of Mobile is Bergeron, *Confederate Mobile*, which chronicles their progress year by year during the war.
5. Andrews, *History of the Campaign of Mobile*, 44; Bergeron, *Confederate Mobile*, 174; O'Brien, *Mobile, 1865*, 44–45, 83–85; Waugh, *Last Stand at Mobile*, 68–77.
6. Jordan, *Operational Art and the Campaigns for Mobile*, 115–22, 130; O'Brien, *Mobile, 1865*, 34; Hansen and Nicolson, *Siege of Blakeley*, 2–10; Waugh, *Last Stand at Mobile*, 68–77; Brueske, *Last Siege*, 22.

7. Bergeron, *Confederate Mobile*, 173–74; Andrews, *History of the Campaign of Mobile*, 31; O'Brien, *Mobile, 1865*, 34–35; Jordan, *Operational Art and the Campaigns for Mobile*, 114–22, Brueske, *Last Siege*, 34.
8. O'Brien, *Mobile, 1865*, 170; Brueske, *Last Siege*, 30, 50; Andrews, *History of the Campaign of Mobile*, 40.
9. Andrews, *History of the Campaign of Mobile*, 33; Brueske, *Last Siege*, 39; O'Brien, *Mobile, 1865*, 57, 61.
10. Report of Brigadier General John P. Hawkins, HQ First Division, USCT, *OR*, series I, part 1, vol. 49, 287; letters of Andrew Lafayette Swap, First Sergeant, 37th Illinois, Nicolson Collection; Bernhardt-Campbell Family Papers, original in Carlisle Barracks Archives; Popchock, *Soldier Boy*, 196; journal of Frederick Pell, 76th Illinois, original in U.S. Army Military Institute at Carlisle Barracks.
11. Andrews, *History of the Campaign of Mobile*, 31, 34–41; Brueske, *Last Siege*, 38, 51; O'Brien, *Mobile, 1865*, 40, 63–64; letters of Major Ephraim Brown, 114th Ohio, April 10 and April 15, 1865, original in Ohio Historical Society; Jonathan Merriam Letters, 117th Illinois, Nicolson Collection.
12. U.S. Census of 1860, available at https://www2.census.gov/library/publications/decennial/1860/population/1860a-04.pdf; Brueske, *Last Siege*, 44, 79; journal of Frederick Pell, 76th Illinois, original in U.S. Army Military Institute at Carlisle Barracks; Scott and Scott, *Montrose*, 28; Scott and Scott, *Daphne*, 204.
13. Andrews, *History of the Campaign of Mobile*, 42–43, 45–47; O'Brien, *Mobile, 1865*, 43–44.
14. Hearn, *Mobile Bay and the Mobile Campaign*, 159–77; Waugh, *Last Stand at Mobile*, 78–85; O'Brien, *Mobile, 1865*, 137–59, 173–84.
15. Benjamin C. Truman, "The Campaign in Alabama," *New York Times*, April 24, 1865, original in Library of Congress.
16. Letters of Major Ephraim Brown, 114th Ohio, April 10 and April 15, 1865, original in Ohio Historical Society; O'Brien, *Mobile, 1865*, 67–68; Rea, "Mississippi Soldier in the Confederacy," 287–89; Andrews, *History of the Campaign of Mobile*, 44.
17. Hearn, *Mobile Bay and the Mobile Campaign*, 178–79; Brueske, *Last Siege*, 80–82; Andrews, *History of the Campaign of Mobile*, 121–23.
18. Lewis to Thomas, April 8, 1865, Liddell Dispatches, Nicolson Collection; Lockett to Ford, April 9, 1865, Garland Collection, Alabama Department of Archives and History.
19. Brueske, *Last Siege*, 48; Lewis to Cockrell, April 1, 1865, Cockrell Dispatches, Nicolson Collection; Lewis to Thomas, April 1, 1865, Cockrell Dispatches, Nicolson Collection.
20. Clark, *Life in the Middle West*, 124; Hill, *History of Company E*, 33.
21. Report of Colonel William T. Spicely, 24th Indiana, *OR*, part I, vol. 49, 209–11; journal of Frederick Pell, 76th Illinois, original in U.S. Army Military Institute at

Carlisle Barracks; Scott, *Story of the Thirty-Second Iowa*, 334–38; Clark; *Life in the Middle West*, 124.

22. Letters of Major Ephraim Brown, 114th Ohio, April 10 and April 15, 1865, original in Ohio Historical Society; Merriam, "Capture of Mobile," vol. 3, 230–50.
23. Scott, *Story of the Thirty-Second Iowa*, 334–38.
24. Lidell Dispatches, April 5 and April 8, 1865, Nicolson Collection.
25. Report of Captain John Murphy, 58th Illinois Infantry, *OR*, part I, vol. 49, 262–63.
26. Civil War and family letters of Private Samuel Crawford, 20th Iowa, Nicolson Collection; Craven, *Brief History of the 89th Indiana*.
27. Letters of Lieutenant Colonel James F. Drish, 122nd Illinois, original in Illinois State Historical Library; journal of Frederick Pell, 76th Illinois, original in U.S. Army Military Institute at Carlisle Barracks; Civil War and family letters of Private Samuel Crawford, 20th Iowa, Nicolson Collection; diary of S.G. Schlagle, 69th Indiana, original in Indiana Historical Society; Churchill, *Geneaology and Biography*, 71–77.
28. Walker *Life of Captain Joseph Fry*, 180–84.
29. Huffstodt, *Hard Dying Men*, 252.
30. Letters of Major Ephraim Brown, 114th Ohio, April 10 and April 15, 1865, original in Ohio Historical Society; Private James M. Dunn with Chesley C. Herndon, "A Diary of Canby's Mobile Campaign, 1865," Nicolson Collection; Report of Colonel William T. Spicely, 24th Indiana, *OR*, part I, vol. 49, 209–11; Lidell to Gibson, Lidell Dispatches, April 5, 1865, Nicolson Collection.
31. Jonathan Merriam Letters, 117th Illinois, Nicolson Collection; Hills, "Last Battle of the War," 181–90; letters of Lieutenant Colonel James F. Drish, 122nd Illinois, original in Illinois State Historical Library; Jones and Dornblaser, *Complete History of the 46th Regiment*, 230–31.
32. Diary of P. Alling, 11th Wisconsin Infantry.
33. Letters of Lieutenant Colonel James F. Drish, 122nd Illinois, original in Illinois State Historical Library; journal of Frederick Pell, 76th Illinois, original in U.S. Army Military Institute at Carlisle Barracks.
34. Civil War and family letters of Private Samuel Crawford, 20th Iowa, Nicolson Collection; journal of Frederick Pell, 76th Illinois, original in U.S. Army Military Institute at Carlisle Barracks.
35. Diary of John Thomas, 47th Indiana, April 1, 2 and 4, 1865, Nicolson Collection; letters of Dolph Wolf, 117th Illinois, April 2, 1865; Nicolson Collection; diary of George Washington Sherman, 27th Iowa, Nicolson Collection.
36. Diary of Avington Wayne Simpson, Nicolson Collection; Thomas Fisher Diary, 11th Illinois, Illinois Civil War Project; letter from Joseph Slagg, 23rd Wisconsin, April 8, 1865, Nicolson Collection.
37. Hills, "Last Battle of the War," 181–90.
38. Letter from Joseph Slagg, 23rd Wisconsin, April 8, 1865, Nicolson Collection.
39. *Mobile Advertiser and Register*, April 9, 1865.

40. O'Brien, *Mobile, 1865*; 180, 185; Report of Major General Edward R.S. Canby, June 1, 1865, *OR*, series I, part 1, vol. 49, 97.
41. Report of General F. Steele, April 17, 1865, *OR*, series I, vol. 49, 283.
42. Henry W. Hart Letters, April 10, 1865, original in Special Collections, Virginia Polytechnic Institute and State University.

Chapter 2

43. James H. Faulkner State Junior College, "The Blakeley Courthouse and Battlefield Investigations: A Preliminary Progress Report," unpublished manuscript, June 30, 1979.
44. Sources consulted for the overview of the fight in this sector of the battlefield include Andrews, *History of the Campaign of Mobile*, 202–11; Blount, *Besieged*, 110–14; Brueske, *Last Siege*, 112–16; Gottschalk, *In Deadly Earnest*, 520–24; Hearn, *Mobile Bay and the Mobile Campaign*, 194–97; and O'Brien, *Mobile, 1865*, 185–206.
45. Henry W. Hart Letters, original in Special Collections, Virginia Polytechnic Institute and State University; Eugene Payne Journal, original in Schoff Civil War Collection, Clements Library, University of Michigan; diary of Corporal William H. Kavanaugh, 2nd and 6th Missouri, original in Missouri Historical Society; letters of Colonel Charles Black, 37th Illinois, original in Illinois State Historical Library.
46. Beyer and Keydel, *Deeds of Valor*, 533–37.
47. Andrews, *History of the Campaign of Mobile*, 203–9.
48. Brigadier General Christopher Columbus, in Andrews, *History of the Campaign of Mobile*, 221.
49. Andrews, *History of the Campaign of Mobile*, 206.
50. Barney, *Recollections of Field Service*.
51. Civil War and family letters of Private Samuel Crawford, 20th Iowa, Nicolson Collection.
52. Dyer, *Compendium of the War of the Rebellion*, 1,062.
53. Eugene Payne Journal, original in Schoff Civil War Collection, Clements Library, University of Michigan.
54. Letter of Colonel Charles Black, April 12, 1865, original in Illinois State Historical Library.
55. Letter from Private T.J. Stow, original at Vicksburg National Military Park.
56. Beyer and Keydel, *Deeds of Valor*, 536–37.
57. Dyer, *Compendium of the War of the Rebellion*, 1,545.
58. Letters of Major Ephraim Brown, 114th Ohio, original in Ohio Historical Society.
59. Dyer, *Compendium of the War of the Rebellion*, 1,535.
60. Gerard, *Diary of the 83rd Ohio Volunteer Infantry*, 64–66.

61. Jackson, *"Some of the Boys,"* 90–96.
62. Dyer, *Compendium of the War of the Rebellion*, 1,179.
63. Clark, *Life in the Middle West*, 125–26.
64. Report of Colonel William T. Spicely, 24th Indiana, *OR*, part I, vol. 49, 209–11.
65. Dyer, *Compendium of the War of the Rebellion*, 1,088.
66. Bilby, "Memoirs of Military Service," 24–29.
67. Report of Lieutenant Colonel Victor Vifquain, 97th Illinois, *OR*, part I, vol. 49, 212–14.
68. Dunn and Herndon, "Diary of Canby's Mobile Campaign, 1865," 6, Nicolson Collection.
69. "Memoir of W.R. Eddington," original in U.S. Army Military History Institute.
70. Dyer, *Compendium of the War of the Rebellion*, 1,144–45.
71. Diary of S.G. Schlagle, 69th Indiana, original in Indiana Historical Society.
72. Martin, "Out of Our Past."
73. Dyer, *Compendium of the War of the Rebellion*, 1,078–79.
74. Report of Colonel S.T. Busey, 76th Illinois, *OR*, part I, vol. 49, 211.
75. *Union Army*, vol. 3, 125.
76. Report of Lieutenant Colonel Francis A Sears, 24th Indiana, *OR*, part I, vol. 49, 214–15.
77. Fulfer, *History of the Trials and Hardships*, 120–21.
78. Dyer, *Compendium of the War of the Rebellion*, 1,007–8.
79. Diary of William J. Gould, original in Library of Congress.
80. Henry W. Hart Letters, original in Special Collections, Virginia Polytechnic Institute and State University.
81. See Gottschalk, *In Deadly Earnest*.
82. National Park Service Battle Unit Details, https://www.nps.gov/civilwar/search-battle-units-detail.htm?battleUnitCode=CMO0002RI01 and https://www.nps.gov/civilwar/search-battle-units-detail.htm?battleUnitCode=CMO0006RI; Root, *Missouri Troops in Service*, 334–35.
83. Diary of Corporal William H. Kavanaugh, 2nd and 6th Missouri Infantry, 38–40, original in State Historical Society of Missouri.
84. National Park Service Battle Unit Details, https://www.nps.gov/civilwar/search-battle-units-detail.htm?battleUnitCode=CMO0001RC01 and https://www.nps.gov/civilwar/search-battle-units-detail.htm?battleUnitCode=CMO0003BC.
85. *Daily Register*, "Brave Men in Distressing Circumstances—A Note About Capt. A.C. Danner," February 16, 1887.
86. Anderson, *Memoirs*, 399.
87. Cleveland, "With the Third Missouri Regiment," *Confederate Veteran Magazine* (January 1923): 20.

Chapter 3

88. O'Brien, *Mobile, 1865*, 90; Hansen and Nicolson, *Siege of Blakeley*, 2. For information on individual units, see https://www.nps.gov/civilwar/search-battle-units.htm.
89. Andrews, *History of the Campaign of Mobile*, 194, 195.
90. Ibid., 196.
91. Ibid., 197.
92. Ibid., 200.
93. Ibid., 200–201.
94. Fitzgerald, "Another Kind of Glory," 260–62; O'Brien, *Mobile, 1865*, 198–99; Brueske, *Last Siege*, 118; Andrews, *History of the Campaign of Mobile*, 200–201.
95. Fitzgerald, "Another Kind of Glory," 243–75; Lardas, "African American Union Troops." For more on the history and organization of the USCT, see Glatthaar, *Forged in Battle*, and Lardas and Dennis, *African-American Soldier in the Civil War*.
96. Report of Brigadier General John P. Hawkins, April 16, 1865, *OR*, part I, vol. 49, 287.
97. National Park Service Battle Unit Details, https://www.nps.gov/civilwar/search-battle-units-detail.htm?battleUnitCode=UUS0073RI00C.
98. Beyer and Keydel, *Deeds of Valor*, 535.
99. Merriam, "Capture of Mobile," vol. 3, 230–50.
100. National Park Service Battle Unit Details, https://www.nps.gov/civilwar/search-battle-units-detail.htm?battleUnitCode=UUS0076RI00C.
101. Report of Colonel Charles W. Drew, April 13, 1865, *OR*, part I, vol. 49, 295–96.
102. National Park Service Battle Unit Details, https://www.nps.gov/civilwar/search-battle-units-detail.htm?battleUnitCode=UUS0047RI00C.
103. Report of Colonel Hiram Scofield, April 11, 1865, *OR*, part I, vol. 49, 290–92.
104. National Park Service Battle Unit Details, https://www.nps.gov/civilwar/search-battle-units-detail.htm?battleUnitCode=UUS0051RI00C.
105. Letter from Walter Chapman to parents, Walter Chapman Papers, original in Yale University Library.
106. Report of Colonel A. Watson Webber, *OR*, part I, vol. 49, 295.
107. National Park Service Battle Unit Details, https://www.nps.gov/civilwar/search-battle-units-detail.htm?battleUnitCode=CMS0004RI01.
108. Bounds, *Ben H. Bounds*, 17–20.
109. Account of Thomas Martin Murphree, Company E, 4th Mississippi Infantry, as recorded by his son, Nicolson Collection.
110. Alabama Department of Archives and History reference files; National Park Service Battle Unit Details, https://www.nps.gov/civilwar/search-battle-units-detail.htm?battleUnitCode=CALTARRYAL.
111. Tarrant, "Siege and Capture of Fort Blakeley," 457–58.

Chapter 4

112. Andrews, *History of the Campaign of Mobile*, 216–17; Report of Brigadier General James I. Gilbert, April 10, 1865, *OR*, part I, vol. 49, 255.
113. Account of Lieutenant Colonel C.S. Hills, *Evening News* (Emporia, KS), June 3, 1865.
114. Andrews, *History of the Campaign of Mobile*, 211.
115. Report of Brigadier General James I. Gilbert, Commanding 2nd Brigade, April 10, 1865, *OR*, part I, vol. 49, 255–56.
116. Dyer, *Compendium of the War of the Rebellion*, 1,188.
117. Report of Lieutenant Colonel Charles S. Hills, April 11, 1865, *OR*, part I, vol. 49, 258–59.
118. *Evening News* (Emporia, KS), June 3, 1865.
119. Dyer, *Compendium of the War of the Rebellion*, 1,178.
120. Scott, *Story of the Thirty-Second Iowa*, 334–38.
121. Dyer, *Compendium of the War of the Rebellion*, 1,176.
122. Reminiscences of Cyrus E. Smith, Company C, 27th Iowa, "Capturing Fort Blakeley: Charging Over the Wire Obstructions, Abatis and Torpedoes—Capturing Rebels and Viewing the Wreck," *National Tribune*, February 3, 1910.
123. Letter from unknown soldier in Company G, 27th Iowa Infantry, May 8, 1865, Nicolson Collection.
124. Dyer, *Compendium of the War of the Rebellion*, 1,096. See also Gerline, *One Hundred Seventeenth Illinois Infantry Volunteers.*
125. Report of Colonel Risdon M. Moore, 117th Illinois Infantry, April 12, 1865, *OR*, part I, vol. 49, 256.
126. Letter of Otto Wolf, 117th Illinois Infantry, April 12, 1865, original in Louisa H. Bowen University Archives and Special Collections Southern Illinois University.
127. Jonathan Merriam Letters, 117th Illinois, Nicolson Collection.
128. Dyer, *Compendium of the War of the Rebellion*, 1,298–99. See also Hill, *History of Company E.*
129. Hill, *History of Company E*, 32–33.
130. Report of Brigadier General James C. Veatch, *OR*, part I, vol. 49, 155–60.
131. Report of General Slack, *OR*, part I, vol. 49, 160–63.
132. Dyer, *Compendium of the War of the Rebellion*, 1,685–86. See also Quiner, *Military History of Wisconsin.*
133. Report of Brigadier General Elias S. Dennis, April 10, 1865, *OR*, part I, vol. 49, 171.
134. Dyer, *Compendium of the War of the Rebellion*, 1,046–47.
135. Report of Colonel Josiah A. Sheetz, *OR*, part I, vol. 49, 175–78.
136. Dyer, *Compendium of the War of the Rebellion*, 1,066–67.
137. Journal of the 46th Illinois Infantry, by Bela St. John, original in Library of Congress.

138. Dyer, *Compendium of the War of the Rebellion*, 1,048–49. See also Huffstodt, *Hard Dying Men.*
139. Thomas Fisher Diary, 11th Illinois, Illinois in the Civil War, https://civilwar.illinoisgenweb.org/scrapbk/fisherdiarylet.html, contributed by Thomas H. Fisher.
140. Account of Lieutenant George D. Carrington in Huffstodt, *Hard Dying Men*, 253.
141. Report of Colonel James. H. Coates, 11th Illinois Infantry, April 20, 1865, *OR*, part I, vol. 49, 180.

Chatper 5

142. Lewis to Cockrell, April 1, 1865, and Lewis to Thomas, April 1, 1865, Cockrell Dispatches, Nicolson Collection.
143. Andrews, *Campaign of Mobile*, 214–15; O'Brien, *Mobile, 1865*, 191.
144. Beyer and Keydel, *Deeds of Valor*, 533–37.
145. Reports of Brigadier General Kenner Garrard, commanding 2nd Division, 16th Army Corps, near Blakeley, April 11, 1865, *OR*, part I, vol. 49, 247–50.
146. Illinois Military and Naval Department, *Report of the Adjutant General of the State of Illinois*, vol. 4, 339–43.
147. Report of Colonel Thomas J. Kinney, 119th Illinois, *OR*, part I, vol. 49, 253–54.
148. Memoirs of L.H. Potts, 119th Illinois, Nicolson Collection.
149. *Deeds of Valor*, 535–36.
150. Diary of First Sergeant Lemuel Burke, Company K, 119th Illinois Infantry, Nicolson Collection.
151. Dyer, *Compendium of the War of the Rebellion*, 1,330–31.
152. Report of Brevet Major and Chief Engineer M.D. McAlester, *OR*, part I, vol. 49, 138–39.
153. Letter of Captain Ed. K. Blackburn, 21st Missouri, to parents of Private Thomas H. Roseberry, Nicolson Collection.
154. Dyer, *Compendium of the War of the Rebellion*, 1,097–98.
155. Report of Colonel John I. Rinaker, 122nd Illinois, Blakeley, April 11, 1865, *OR*, part I, vol. 49, 250–53.
156. Letters of Lieutenant Colonel James F. Drish, 122nd Illinois, original in Illinois State Historical Library.
157. Letter of Private William H. Peter, Company D, 122nd Illinois Infantry, Nicolson Collection.
158. Dyer, *Compendium of the War of the Rebellion*, 1,151.
159. Report of Lieutenant Colonel Hervey Craven, 89th Indiana, April 10, 1865, Craven, *Brief History of the 89th Indiana.*
160. Dyer, *Compendium of the War of the Rebellion*, 1,072–73.
161. Report of Captain John Murphy, 58th Illinois Infantry, Fort Blakeley, April 10, 1865, *OR*, part I, vol. 49, 262–63.

162. Dyer, *Compendium of the War of the Rebellion*, 1,469.
163. Report of Lieutenant Colonel John R. Gandolfo, 178th New York Infantry, April 10, 1865, *OR*, part I, vol. 49, 265.
164. Dyer, *Compendium of the War of the Rebellion*, 1,677–78.
165. Report of Major Jesse S. Miller, 11th Wisconsin Infantry, April 10, 1865, *OR*, part I, vol. 49, 266.
166. Report of Colonel Charles L. Harris, 11th Wisconsin Infantry, April 10, 1865, *OR*, part I, vol. 49, 260–62.
167. Dyer, *Compendium of the War of the Rebellion*, 1,365.
168. Report of Colonel William Hudson Lawrence, 34th New Jersey Infantry, April 10, 1865, *OR*, part I, vol. 49, 264–65.
169. Dyer, *Compendium of the War of the Rebellion*, 1,139.
170. Report of Lieutenant Colonel Zalmon S. Main, 52nd Indiana, Fort Blakeley, April 10, 1865, *OR*, part I, vol. 49, 263–64.
171. Alabama Department of Archives and History Reference Files. See also Brewer, *Brief Historical Sketches of Military Organizations*, 229–31.
172. Asa M. Piper, "Some Recollections of an Old Soldier," unpublished manuscript, Company C, 62nd Alabama Volunteers, Nicolson Collection.
173. Hughes, *Lidell's Record*, 196.
174. Watson considerably overestimated the strength of the Union forces assaulting Blakeley and the casualties they incurred in his account and accidentally inflated by a small margin the number of Confederates present. James Thomas Jefferson Watson, "Statement of My War Record," Nicolson Collection.

Chapter 6

175. Information on the historic town of Blakeley taken from Hamilton, *Colonial Mobile*, 397–98; Harris, *Dead Towns of Alabama*, 63–65; Nuzum, *History of Baldwin County*, 69–76; and Mary Y. Grice, "The Dead City of Blakeley," unpublished manuscript in research files of Historic Blakeley State Park.
176. Lieutenant George Warren Diary, Nicolson Collection.
177. McClellan, "Vivid Reminiscences of War Times," 265. The batteries firing on Spanish Fort that McClellan refers to were probably Batteries Huger and Tracy.
178. Bevier, *History of the First and Second Missouri*, 265–67.
179. Report of Lieutenant Bennett, commanding CSS *Nashville*, *OR*, part I, vol. 49, 319–22.
180. Cameron, "Battles Opposite Mobile," 305–7.
181. Gerard, *Diary of the 83rd Ohio Volunteer Infantry*, 71–72.
182. Johnson, *Muskets and Medicine*, 220.

Bibliography

Archives

Alabama Department of Archives and History.
Library of Congress.
Nicolson Collection, Historic Mobile Preservation Society.

Published Sources

Anderson, Ephraim McDonald. *Memoirs: Historical and Personal; Including the Campaigns of the First Missouri Confederate Brigade*. St. Louis, MO: Times Printing Company, 1868.

Andrews, Christopher C. *History of the Campaign of Mobile*. New York: D. Van Nostrand, 1889.

Barney, Chester. *Recollections of Field Service with the 20th Iowa Infantry*. Davenport, IA: Gazette Job Rooms, 1865.

Bergeron, Arthur W., Jr. *Confederate Mobile*. Baton Rouge: Louisiana State University Press, 1991.

Bevier, R.S. *History of the First and Second Missouri Confederate Brigades, 1861–1865*. St. Louis, MO: Bryan, Brand and Company, 1879.

Beyer, Walter F., and Oscar F. Keydel, eds. *Deeds of Valor: How America's Heroes Won the Medal of Honor*. Detroit, MI: Perrien-Keydel Company, 1901.

Bilby, Joseph G., ed. "Memoirs of Military Service, Carlos W. Colby, Co. G, 97th Illinois Infantry." *Military Images* 3, no. 2 (1981).

Blount, Russell W., Jr. *Besieged: Mobile 1865*. Gretna, LA: Pelican Publishing, 2015.

Bounds, Charles L., ed. *Ben H. Bounds, 1840–1911, Methodist Minister and Prominent Mason: Biography and Highlights from His Early Life and Civil War Memoirs.* Columbus, OH: J.O. Moore, 1962.

Brewer, Willis. *Brief Historical Sketches of Military Organizations Formed in Alabama during the Civil War*. Montgomery, Alabama Department of Archives and History, 1966.

Brueske, Paul. *The Last Siege: The Mobile Campaign, Alabama 1865*. Oxford, UK: Casemate, 2018.

Buel, Clarence Clough, and Robert Underwood Johnson. *Battles and Leaders of the Civil War*. Vol. 4, *Retreat with Honor*. Secaucus, NJ: Castle, 2010.

Cameron, William Lochiel. "The Battles Opposite Mobile." *Confederate Veteran Magazine* 23, no. 7 (1915): 305–7.

Churchill, Samuel J. *Geneaology and Biography of the Connecticut Branch of the Churchill Family in America*. Lawrence, KS: Journal Publishing, 1901.

Clark, J.S. *Life in the Middle West: Reminiscences of J.S. Clark*. Chicago: Advance, 1916.

Cleveland, Charles Boarman. "With the Third Missouri Regiment." *Confederate Veteran Magazine* (January 1923): 20.

Craven, Hervey. *A Brief History of the 89th Indiana Volunteer Infantry, From Its Organization August 28, 1862, to the Close of Its Term of Service, Including Official Reports, and a List of Casualties in Action*. Wabash, IN, 1877.

Dyer, Frederick H. *A Compendium of the War of the Rebellion*. Des Moines, IA: Dyer Publishing Company, 1908.

Farragut, Loyall. *The Life of David Glasgow Farragut*. New York: D. Appleton, 1879.

Fitzgerald, Michael W. "Another Kind of Glory: Black Participation and Its Consequences in the Campaign for Confederate Mobile," *Alabama Review* 54 (October 2001): 243–75.

Fulfer, Richard J. *A History of the Trials and Hardships of the Twenty-Fourth Indiana Volunteer Infantry*. Indianapolis, IN: Indianapolis Printing Company, 1913.

Gerard, C.W. *A Diary of the 83rd Ohio Volunteer Infantry in the War, 1862–1865*. Cincinnati, OH, 1890.

Gerline, Edwin G. *The One Hundred Seventeenth Illinois Infantry Volunteers (The McKendree Regiment): 1862–1865*. Highland, IL: E.G. Gerling, 1992.

Glatthaar, Joseph T. *Forged in Battle: The Civil War Alliance of Black Soldiers and White Officers*. Baton Rouge: Louisiana State University Press, 1990.

Gottschalk, Phil. *In Deadly Earnest: The Missouri Brigade*. Columbia: Missouri River Press, 1991.

Gue, Benjamin F. *History of Iowa from the Earliest Times to the Beginning of the Twentieth Century*. New York: Century History Company, 1903.

Hamilton, Peter. *Colonial Mobile*. New York: Houghton, Mifflin and Company, 1898.

Hansen, Roger B., and Norman A. Nicolson. *The Siege of Blakeley and the Campaign of Mobile: The Final Days of the Last Major Battle of the Civil War Fought at Fort Blakeley, Alabama, April 9, 1865*. Spanish Fort, AL: Historic Blakeley Press, 1995.

Harris, W. Stuart. *Dead Towns of Alabama.* Tuscaloosa: University of Alabama Press, 1977.

Hearn, Chester G. *Mobile Bay and the Mobile Campaign: The Last Great Battles of the Civil War.* Jefferson, NC: McFarland and Company, 1998.

Hill, Alfred J. *A History of Company E of the Sixth Minnesota Regiment of Volunteer Infantry.* St. Paul: Pioneer Press Company, 1899.

Hills, Charles S. "The Last Battle of the War: Recollections of the Mobile Campaign." In *War Papers and Person Reminiscences.* Vol. 1, *1861–65.* St. Louis, MO: Becktold, 1892.

History of Huntington County, Indiana, From the Earliest Time to the Present. Chicago: Brant and Fuller, 1887.

History of Macoupin County, Illinois, with Illustrations Descriptive of Its Scenery, and Biographical Sketches of Some of Its Prominent Men and Pioneers. Philadelphia, PA: Brink, McDonough and Company, 1879.

History of Madison County, Indiana, with Illustrations and Biographical Sketches of Some of Its Prominent Men and Pioneers. Chicago: Kingman Brothers, 1880.

Huffstodt, Jim. *Hard Dying Men: The Story of General W.H.L. Wallace, General T.E.G. Ransom, and Their "Old Eleventh" Illinois Infantry in the American Civil War 1861–1865.* Bowie, MD: Heritage Books, 1991.

Hughes, Nathaniel Cheirs, Jr., ed. *Liddell's Record.* Baton Rouge: Louisiana State University Press, 1985.

Illinois Military and Naval Department. *Report of the Adjutant General of the State of Illinois for the Years 1861–1866.* Vol. 6. Springfield, IL: Journal Company, 1900.

Jackson, Joseph O., ed. *"Some of the Boys": The Civil War Letters of Isaac Jackson, 1862–1865.* Carbondale: Southern Illinois University Press, 1960.

Johnson, Charles B. *Muskets and Medicine, or Army Life in the Sixties.* Philadelphia, PA: F.A. Davis, 1917.

Jones, Thomas B., and Benjamin Dornblaser. *Complete History of the 46th Regiment, Illinois Volunteer Infantry.* Freeport, IL: W.H. Wagner and Sons, 1900.

Jordan, Daniel W., III. *Operational Art and the Campaigns for Mobile, 1864–65: A Staff Ride Handbook.* Fort Leavenworth, KS: Combat Studies Institute, 2019.

Lanier, Robert S. *The Photographic History of the Civil War in Ten Volumes.* Vol. 10, *Armies and Leaders.* New York: Review of Reviews Company, 1911.

Lardas, Mark, and Peter Dennis. *African-American Soldier in the Civil War (USCT) 1862–1866.* Oxford, UK: Osprey Publishing, 2006.

Martin, Steve. "Out of Our Past: Final Battle of the Civil War Involved Men from Wayne County." *Richmond Palladium-Item*, April 8, 2018.

McClellan, Alden. "Vivid Reminiscences of War Times." *Confederate Veteran Magazine* (June 1906): 265.

Merriam, Henry C. "The Capture of Mobile." In *Military Order of the Loyal Legion of the United States* 3 (1905).

Noles, Jim. "Confederate Twilight: The Fall of Fort Blakeley." *Alabama Heritage* (Winter 2009): 28–37.

Nuzum, Kay. *A History of Baldwin County*. Fairhope, AL: Page & Palette, 1971.

O'Brien, Sean Michael. *Mobile, 1865: Last Stand of the Confederacy.* Westport, CT: Praeger, 2001.

Popchock, Barry. *Soldier Boy: The Civil War Letters of Charles O. Musser, 29th Iowa*. Iowa City: University of Iowa Press, 1995.

Quiner, E.B. *The Military History of Wisconsin: A Record of the Civil and Military Patriotism of the State in the War for the Union.* Chicago: Clarke and Company, 1866.

Rea, Captain R.N. "Mississippi Soldier in the Confederacy." *Confederate Veteran Magazine* 30 (n.d.): 287–89.

Root, Elihu. *Missouri Troops in Service during the Civil War*. Washington, D.C.: Government Printing Office, 1902.

Scott, Florence D'Olive, and Richard Joseph Scott. *Daphne: A History of Its People and Their Pursuits as Some Saw It and Others Rremember It.* Montgomery, AL: Paragon, 1965.

———. *Montrose: As It Was Recorded, Told About, and Lived.* Montgomery, AL: Paragon, 1976.

Scott, John. *The Story of the Thirty-Second Iowa Infantry Volunteers*. Nevada, IA: John Scott, 1896.

Tarrant, E.W. "Siege and Capture of Fort Blakeley." *Confederate Veteran Magazine* (October 1915): 457–58.

Trudeau, Noah Andre. *Out of the Storm: The End of the Civil War, April–June 1865*. New York: Little, Brown and Company, 1994.

The Union Army: A History of Military Affairs in the Loyal States, 1861–1865. Vol. 3. Madison, WI: Federal Publishing Company, 1908.

U.S. War Department. *The War of the Rebellion: A Compilation of the Official Records of the Union and Confederate Armies*. Washington, D.C.: Government Printing Office, 1880–1901.

Walker, Jeanie Mort. *Life of Captain Joseph Fry, The Cuban Martyr*. Hartford, CT: J.B. Burr Publishing, 1874.

Waugh, John C. *Last Stand at Mobile*. Abilene, TX: McWhiney Foundation, 2001.

Witherspoon, Halliday. *Men of Illinois*. Chicago: H. Witherspoon, 1902.

Online Resources

Illinois Civil War Project, https://civilwar.illinoisgenweb.org.

Mark N. Lardas, "African American Union Troops," http://www.encyclopediaofalabama.org/article/h-2022.

National Park Service Civil War Database, https://www.nps.gov/civilwar/index.htm.

About the Author

Mike Bunn is a historian and author who has worked with several cultural heritage organizations in the Southeast. He currently serves as director of Historic Blakeley State Park in Spanish Fort, Alabama. He is author or coauthor of several books, including *Fourteenth Colony: The Forgotten Story of the Gulf South during America's Revolutionary Era*; *Early Alabama: An Illustrated Guide to the Formative Years, 1798–1826*; *Alabama from Territory to Statehood: An Alabama Heritage Bicentennial Collection*; *Well Worth Stopping to See: Antebellum Columbus, Georgia through the Eyes of Travelers*; *Civil War Eufaula*; *Battle for the Southern Frontier: The Creek War and the War of 1812*; and *The Lower Chattahoochee River* (Images of America). Mike earned his undergraduate degree at Faulkner University and two master's degrees at the University of Alabama. He and his wife, Tonya, live in Daphne, Alabama, with their daughter, Zoey. www.mikebunn.net.